THE QUICK AND EASY RAW FOOD COOKBOOK

The Quick and Easy Raw Food Cookbook

by Moira Hodgson

GROSSET & DUNLAP
A NATIONAL GENERAL COMPANY
Publishers *New York*

I am indebted to Victor di Suvero who had the original idea for this book one afternoon in Santa Fe.

My thanks go to my grandmother, Mrs. H. O. Hamilton, my mother, to Raeford Liles, and to Bill, who all helped inspire recipes and ideas for this book.

PUBLISHED BY GROSSET & DUNLAP, INC.
PUBLISHED SIMULTANEOUSLY IN CANADA.
LIBRARY OF CONGRESS CATALOG CARD NUMBER: 74-145730
ISBN: 0-448-02436-5

Printed in the United States of America

Contents

Soups

A cold soup is as excellent a light beginning to a summer meal as it is to a hearty dinner. In the making of fresh homemade soups the blender has virtually saved the life of the cook. In the past, homemade cold soups involved hours of preparation; nowadays it is a simple matter to peel vegetables and blend them for a few seconds with the other ingredients.

The soup should be well chilled before it is served and if you leave it overnight in the refrigerator the flavor will have ample time to develop. A scattering of fresh herbs or paprika over the top of the soup, or a little fresh cream poured into it when ready to serve, will both add to its looks and enhance its flavor.

Avocado Soup with Chives

2 ripe avocados
2 minced scallions
1 tablespoon lemon juice
1 cup yoghurt
½ cup light cream
1 cup cold chicken broth
dash curry powder
kosher salt and freshly ground black pepper
2 tablespoons chopped chives

Peel and pit the avocados, mash and put them in a blender. Add the rest of the ingredients except the chives. (If you do not have a blender, work the ingredients into the avocado until you have a thick soup.) Adjust the seasonings and chill. When ready to serve, sprinkle the chives over the top of each serving. Serves 4.

Avocado Cream Soup

2 ripe avocados
1 cup chicken broth (cold)
½ cup sour cream
½ cup heavy cream
1 tablespoon lemon juice
dash Worcestershire sauce
kosher salt and freshly ground black pepper
paprika
optional: ¼ cup pale dry sherry

Combine all ingredients except paprika in blender (or mash in bowl). Chill, adjust seasoning, and sprinkle paprika over the top of each serving as decoration. Serves 4.

Jellied Avocado Soup

2 cans consommé madrilene
1 large ripe avocado
1 cup sour cream
2 tablespoons finely chopped onion
½ teaspoon chili powder
juice of half a lemon
kosher salt and freshly ground black pepper
fresh chopped dill
paprika

Combine consommé with chopped avocado, onion, chili, lemon juice, sour cream, and seasonings. Chill until jellied. Place in individual bowls, top with dill and paprika, and serve. Serves 4.

Cold Buttermilk Soup

This is good either as a dessert or for a light summer luncheon.

3 egg yolks
½ cup raw sugar
juice of 1 lemon
¼ teaspoon lemon rind
1 teaspoon vanilla (optional)
1 quart buttermilk
1 cup heavy cream
½ cup chopped almonds
raspberry jam (or fresh raspberries)

In a bowl beat the egg yolks, sugar, and lemon juice. Add the lemon rind and vanilla and gradually beat in the buttermilk. Chill (must be very cold). To serve add heavy cream, chopped almonds, and raspberry jam (just a small spoonful to each serving) without mixing in. Serves 6.

Yoghurt and Cucumber Soup

2 cucumbers
2 cups yoghurt
1 tablespoon white or tarragon vinegar
1 teaspoon lemon juice
1 tablespoon olive oil
2 tablespoons fresh chopped dill
kosher salt and freshly ground black pepper

Peel the cucumbers and either grate as finely as you can or put them, coarsely sliced, into the blender. Put the yoghurt in a large mixing bowl and gradually stir in the cucumber puree, the vinegar, lemon juice, oil, and about ¾ of the chopped dill. Season and chill for an hour. When ready to serve scatter the remaining dill over the top of each serving. Serves 4. (For best results, use home-made yoghurt.)

Jellied Cucumber Soup

This is a good summer soup equally welcome at lunch or dinner. Serve it in individual soup bowls with chopped mint sprinkled over the top.

2 large cucumbers
½ pint aspic jelly or one can jellied consommé
juice of half a lemon
1 tablespoon grated onion
kosher salt and white pepper
1 teaspoon fresh chopped mint (no substitute)

Peel and grate the cucumbers. Salt and let sit for about an hour. Meanwhile prepare the aspic jelly. Dry the cucumbers and combine in a large bowl with the aspic, lemon, onion, and seasonings. Refrigerate until set (about three hours). Spoon the jelly into individual bowls and serve at once (do not leave the soup on the table while you round up the diners, particularly if it is summer time — the soup starts to melt immediately) with mint scattered over the top. Serves 4.

Cucumber Soup with Mint or Dill

2 large cucumbers
½ pint sour cream
4 scallions
1 teaspoon lemon juice
kosher salt and freshly ground black pepper
2 tablespoons fresh chopped mint or dill

Peel the cucumbers and either grate them as finely as you can or put them, coarsely sliced, into the blender. In a large bowl combine the puree with the sour cream. Slice the scallions finely, using both the white and green part, and add to the mixture. Add the lemon juice and seasonings. Serve in individual bowls with mint or dill scattered on top or in a large serving bowl with most of the herb mixed in, a little reserved for the top. Serves 4.

Jellied Madrilene with Red Caviar

2 cans consommé madrilene
2 ounces red caviar
juice of half a lemon
6 tablespoons sour cream
3 teaspoons minced chives
black pepper

Chill consommé and place in four individual soup bowls. Top each serving with caviar, lemon juice, sour cream, chives, and pepper and serve. Serves 4.

Note: When fresh chives are not available you can get frozen ones which keep for months in the freezer. Just take the amount you need without ever unfreezing. Or use the freeze-dried variety.

Gazpacho

This is a famous Spanish soup and there are endless variations upon it. Here is one of the recipes that I like best.

2 tomatoes, peeled and with seeds removed (dropping them briefly into boiling water facilitates peeling)
2 cucumbers, peeled
1 medium onion, coarsely chopped
2 cloves garlic
1 tablespoon olive oil
½ teaspoon cumin
1 tablespoon freshly chopped basil
1 sweet red pepper, coarsely chopped
dash Tabasco sauce
1 cup heavy cream
kosher salt and freshly ground black pepper

In blender place ingredients a little at a time, and blend until smooth. Reserve half the cream to pour into the soup when you serve it. Pour the cold soup into individual bowls and top with cream. Then let everyone help themselves to garnish. Serves 4.

Garnish

1 hard-boiled egg, chopped
½ tomato, chopped
1 tablespoon parsley, chopped
croutons
2 tablespoons chopped cucumber

Spanish Tomato Soup

4 large ripe tomatoes
2 onions, coarsely chopped
1 teaspoon sugar
2 tablespoons dry red wine
kosher salt and freshly ground black pepper
1 clove garlic
1 teaspoon paprika
2 tablespoons olive oil
¼ pound black Greek olives
1 teaspoon fresh chopped parsley

Peel the tomatoes (dropping them briefly in boiling water will facilitate peeling) and place them in blender with the onions and the wine. Add the sugar and seasonings and blend at high speed for a few seconds, or until the mixture has become pureed. Squeeze the garlic into a bowl, add the paprika, and mix well. Gradually add the oil until the mixture becomes a creamy paste. Add to the blender and blend in. Pit, chop, and reserve the olives. Chill the soup for at least two hours. When ready to serve, scatter the olives and parsley over the top. Serves 4.

Cold Tomato Soup

3 cups tomato juice
2 tablespoons tomato paste
4 minced scallions (including tops)
1 tablespoon freshly chopped basil
½ teaspoon powdered (or fresh, if available) thyme
dash curry powder
dash Worcestershire sauce
dash Tabasco sauce
dash sugar
1 teaspoon grated lemon rind
juice of 1 lemon
1 cup sour cream
kosher salt and freshly ground black pepper
2 teaspoons chopped parsley

Mix ingredients together, reserving half of the sour cream and the parsley for later use. Chill the soup. When ready to serve, place in individual bowls, put a spoonful of sour cream in each bowl, and scatter parsley over the top. Serves 4.

Watercress Soup

2 cans chicken stock
2 bunches watercress, stalks cut off
juice of half a lemon
1 tablespoon chopped onion
1 cup yoghurt
½ cup heavy cream
kosher salt and freshly ground black pepper

Put all the ingredients in the blender (you will probably have to do this in two shifts) and blend until smooth. Refrigerate the soup until ready to serve. Garnish with pieces of watercress, some extra cream, and a paper-thin slice of lemon. Serves 4–6.

Hors d'Oeuvres and Smorgasbords

Traditionally hors d'oeuvres are light and delicate and serve to stimulate the appetite in anticipation of the main meal. While the name "hors d'oeuvre" is French, these delicacies are also found in other countries under other names. In Italy, for example, they are called *antipasto*, in Russia *zakuski* (always accompanied by plenty of vodka), and in Sweden, *smörgåsbord.* In each case they include green vegetables (such as celery and fennel), pieces of cheese, and raw or smoked fish or meat.

The smörgåsbord in Sweden has now become a main meal in which hot and cold, raw and cooked dishes are included in a magnificent spread set out on a long table. Raw foods are excellent in this context, providing a balance with the heavy foods, and helping stimulate the appetite for more.

To display these dishes most attractively, make liberal use of parsley, radishes, tomato, and lemon slices.

Avocado

The avocado is one of the most delicious and happily one of the most nourishing of fruits. It is high in protein and vitamins yet low in carbohydrates. To test whether an avocado is ripe, press it at the small end. It should be soft. If there are blackish patches inside, don't be put off — they don't taste bad. Lemon squeezed over the meat stops it from going brown. You can buy avocados hard and let them ripen. I've found this to work very well in most cases, although once in a while I've come across a dud that rotted before it ripened. If you plant the stone you might get a beautiful plant.

I prefer to eat avocado plain, with lemon and perhaps a little olive oil — filling it with crabmeat and such hides the taste of the avocado and does not do justice to the seafood.

Serve avocado at room temperature.

Avocado with Chervil

2 avocados
juice of 1 lemon
kosher salt and freshly ground pepper
2 tablespoons of chervil, coarsley chopped
dash paprika (for decoration)

Slice the peeled avocado thin and squeeze the lemon over the slices, making sure that you have covered it well or it will go brown. Refrigerate, turning it from time to time. Just before serving, season the avocado and sprinkle the chervil and paprika over the slices. Serves 4.

Guacamole

2 large avocados
4 ounces cream cheese
1 small onion, finely chopped
juice of half a lemon
dash Tabasco sauce
½ teaspoon chili powder
kosher salt, freshly ground black pepper

If you have a blender you will save yourself plenty of time and trouble. Peel the avocados and put in blender with the other ingredients. Blend and adjust seasoning. Place mixture in bowl and squeeze lemon juice over the top to stop the mixture from going brown.

Cauliflower with Curry Dip

1 head cauliflower, washed and broken into flowerets

Sauce

½ cup mayonnaise (preferably, homemade)
½ teaspoon curry powder
dash cumin
kosher salt and freshly ground pepper
squeeze lemon juice
paprika

Mix all ingredients in bowl. Adjust seasoning and serve as dip for cauliflower, with paprika scattered over the top.

Celery Stuffed with Cream Cheese

1 head celery
1 cup cream cheese
1 teaspoon caraway seeds
½ cup pimiento-stuffed green olives
kosher salt and freshly ground black pepper
cayenne pepper

Remove the stalks from the celery and trim them, removing the leaves, etc. In a bowl combine the cheese and caraway seeds. Slice the olives thinly and add them to the mixture. Season and stuff into the celery stalks. Scatter paprika over the top and serve. Enough for about 4 people as an appetizer.

Endive Stuffed with Roquefort Cheese

2 medium-sized endives
½ cup Roquefort cheese
¼ cup heavy cream
freshly ground black pepper
lemon juice

Pull the leaves off the endives. Wipe (do not wash) them and squeeze a little lemon juice over them. Mix the cheese with the cream and stuff the leaves with the mixture, sprinkling the whole with black pepper and garnishing with black olives, halved baby tomatoes or the like. Can be used as an appetizer (serves 4) or as an hors d'oeuvre for a party.

Mushroom Appetizer

Raw mushrooms have much more flavor than cooked ones. This

appetizer has a piquant flavor, but it is not so strong as to overwhelm the taste of the mushrooms.

½ pound fresh white mushrooms
2 tablespoons olive oil
½ teaspoon chili powder
juice of 1 lemon
dash curry powder
1 teaspoon prepared horseradish
2 drops Tabasco sauce
dash Worcestershire sauce
kosher salt and freshly ground black pepper
fresh chopped parsley for decoration

Slice the mushrooms, reserving the stems for cooking at another time. In a bowl combine the sauce ingredients and adjust the seasoning. Toss the mushrooms in the sauce and refrigerate overnight (or at least for a few hours). When ready to serve, either place in individual dishes or in a large bowl, with chopped parsley sprinkled over the top for decoration. Serves 4.

Mushrooms with Green Garlic Stuffing

These make an excellent beginning to a dinner and you can prepare them the day before, since they improve on being left overnight.

1 pound (about 16) large mushrooms
2 cloves garlic
1 tablespoon spinach leaves
1 tablespoon chopped parsley
1 tablespoon watercress
1 teaspoon chives
1 teaspoon Dijon mustard
2 tablespoons dry red wine or tarragon vinegar
½-¾ cup olive oil
kosher salt and freshly ground black pepper

Remove the stalks from the mushrooms and reserve for cooking at another time. In a bowl squeeze the garlic (or chop it very fine if you do not have a garlic squeezer). Chop the vegetables very fine (use scissors and chop them in a cup) and add to the garlic. Add the rest of the ingredients, check seasoning, and stuff the mixture into the mushroom caps which you then place, upside down, on a plate. Refrigerate until ready to serve. The liquid from the mixture will be seeped up by the mushrooms, enhancing their flavor. Serves 4.

Mushrooms Stuffed with Roquefort Cheese

Mushrooms and cheese are an excellent combination. This can be served either at a cocktail party or to begin a meal.

- 12 mushroom caps
- ½ pound Roquefort cheese
- freshly ground black pepper
- 2 tablespoons chopped chives

Fill the mushroom caps with the cheese, crack a little black pepper over the top, and scatter the chives over the mixture.

Anchovies in Oil

This dish makes a simple and attractive item in a smorgasbord or buffet dinner. You can add all kinds of raw vegetables (such as tomatoes, cauliflower, lettuce leaves, etc.) to make the dish larger or more attractive.

- 3 cans anchovies
- finely chopped white of two hard-boiled eggs
- 1 red pepper, chopped
- 1 tablespoon finely chopped fresh parsley
- kosher salt and freshly ground black pepper to taste
- olive oil (use a strong Spanish or Italian oil)

Lay the anchovy halves on a plate and garnish with the egg white, pepper, and parsley. Season and pour over the oil.

Stuffed Anchovies

Buy dried anchovies, not those that are canned in oil. The dried ones are very salty, hence the soaking in white wine. For an attractive effect, slice some pimientos very thin, and place a sliver across each rolled anchovy.

- 2 cups dry white wine
- 24 (approximately) anchovy fillets
- 1 cup breadcrumbs (preferably from dark bread)
- 1 egg yolk
- 2 tablespoons parsley
- ½ teaspoon cumin
- dash cayenne
- dash curry powder
- 2 tablespoons chopped pimientos
- freshly ground black pepper
- kosher salt to taste

Soak the anchovy fillets overnight in white wine, turning occasionally. In a bowl mix the other ingredients. If too moist add more breadcrumbs. Shape the mixture into balls and wind an anchovy fillet around each one. Place on large plate and decorate with slivers of pimiento over the top. Makes 24.

Anchovy and Olive Canapés

These canapés are very easy to make. You can either place sliced olives over the mixture on the bread, or, if the olives are large enough, you can stuff them with it. The black Greek olives are too salty for the anchovies and the canned black olives, to my mind, have no taste. I find the best kind to use are large green Spanish olives. Be sure to spread a thin layer of butter on the bread before you put the mixture on it — this prevents the bread from getting soggy.

- 3 cans anchovies
- 3 tablespoons fresh chopped parsley
- 2 tablespoons chopped onion
- ½ teaspoon cayenne pepper
- freshly ground black pepper to taste
- 1 egg yolk
- butter (unsalted)
- dark bread (black or pumpernickel)

Chop the anchovies up and either pound them in a mortar or put them in a blender with their oil and the other ingredients. Season. Cut and butter small rounds of bread and place the mixture on top. Top with olive slices and serve.

Note: a little extra cayenne pepper sprinkled over the canapés helps make them look more attractive.

Fågelbo (Bird's Nest)

This is an old Swedish recipe, and is good either as an hors d'oeuvre or in smorgasbord.

- 8 Swedish anchovy fillets
- 1 tablespoon chopped raw onion
- 1 tablespoon capers
- 1 tablespoon chopped fresh chives
- 1 tablespoon diced pickled beets (optional)
- 1 tablespoon cold diced boiled potatoes (optional)
- 2 egg yolks

Arrange the anchovy fillets in rings with the egg yolks in the center. Arrange the onion, capers, chives, beets, and potatoes around. The first person to help himself stirs all the ingredients together. Serves 4.

Caviar

Always serve caviar thoroughly chilled. You can serve it on thin slices of toast, buttered or plain, with lemon slices on the side. It can also be served with blintzes, melted butter, and sour cream. Caviar and cream cheese with sour cream on slices of fresh black bread is also delicious.

There is no particular wine that goes with caviar. The most common drinks are Champagne or stout.

Black Caviar with Hard-Boiled Eggs

Danish caviar is good in this combination. Serve with hot toast.

⅔ cup heavy cream
3 tablespoons black caviar
1½ tablespoons chopped onion
2 hard-boiled eggs

Whip the cream, stir in the caviar and onion. Place it in a mound in the middle of a dish and garnish with sliced eggs.

Tomatoes Stuffed with Caviar and Sour Cream

This recipe is delicious either as an hors d'oeuvre or served on a side dish with salad. Peel the tomatoes by dropping them into boiling water.

I am indebted to my mother for this dish.

6 medium-sized tomatoes, peeled
1 small jar Danish caviar
about 2 teaspoons sour cream
squeeze of lemon juice
freshly ground black pepper

Halve the tomatoes and scoop out the insides. Mix the caviar gently with the sour cream, taking care not to put in too much cream or it will get mushy. Squeeze a little lemon juice to taste into the mixture. Grind some pepper into the tomato halves and fill with the caviar mixture. Makes 12 halves.

Red Caviar with Hard-Boiled Eggs

6 hard-boiled eggs
1 small onion, finely chopped
6 tablespoons melted butter
1 4-ounce jar red caviar
1 cup sour cream
kosher salt and freshly ground black pepper
finely chopped chives
black bread or thin rye toast

Chop the hard-boiled eggs and combine in bowl with onions, melted butter, caviar, and sour cream. Season. Place mixture on slices of bread or toast, thinly buttered to prevent the moisture from dampening the bread, and scatter chives over the top. Serve with lemon slices.

Red Caviar with Japanese Dressing

Use the large white radish which is available in Chinese or Japanese stores. If this is not available substitute icicle radish or small white turnips.

½ pound Japanese radish
1 4-ounce jar red caviar
juice of half a lemon
freshly ground white pepper
parsley sprigs
lemon wedges

Peel and grate the radish finely. Add the lemon juice and white pepper. Carefully fold in the red caviar and serve garnished with parsley sprigs and lemon wedges. Serves 4.

Note: You can also add a little soy sauce to the mixture or serve it separately.

Clams

I personally best like clams served raw in their shells with lemon and black pepper. However, I have included some recipes for clams served in various sauces for those who like variety.

Clam Cocktail

- 2 dozen clams, with juice
- 2 large ripe tomatoes, peeled, seeded, and chopped
- 1 small green chili pepper
- ½ tablespoon parsley, coarsely chopped
- dash sugar
- 1 egg yolk
- 2 tablespoons olive oil
- dash Worcestershire sauce
- 1 teaspoon fresh grated horseradish
- juice of half a lemon
- kosher salt and cayenne pepper
- 1 clove garlic, sliced

Shell the clams, reserving the juice, and place in bowl with garlic. Combine the tomatoes with the chili, parsley, sugar, and salt and pepper, add the clam juice, and beat in the egg yolk. Gradually add the oil and remaining seasonings. Turn the clams from time to time and remove the garlic before serving. Serve in individual dishes, either 6 or 12 per person.

Clam Dip

Use this dip on open-faced sandwiches (try it on black bread) or as a dip for vegetables such as raw celery.

- 1 cup clams, with juice
- juice of 1 lemon
- 1 teaspoon lemon rind, grated
- 2 teaspoons freshly chopped parsley
- dash Worcestershire sauce
- dash Tabasco sauce
- dash chili powder
- dash dry mustard
- 1 cup cream cheese
- dash curry powder
- kosher salt and freshly ground black pepper
- 1 teaspoon chopped fresh chives to garnish (optional)

In the blender put all the ingredients except the chives. Blend at high speed and taste for seasoning. Adjust spices depending on how you like it. Refrigerate the dip until ready to use. Sprinkle the chives over when spread on bread, or in bowl. Enough for about 24 small open-faced sandwiches or canapés.

Oysters

Oysters are best served cold in their shells. To prepare them, run them lightly under cold water and place them, preferably over crushed ice, on a plate in the half shell. Cayenne or freshly ground black pepper and lemon slices are traditional accompaniments.

Some people like to serve them with horseradish and tomato sauce, but to my mind this overpowers the delicate flavor of the oysters.

Oysters have a high iodine content and are good for people suffering from anemia. Eat them during the months with an "r" in their name — sometimes they can be dangerous when eaten during the summer and anyway they need a chance to breed.

Oysters go particularly well with a cold Chablis or with stout.

Sauce for Raw Oysters

I prefer oysters plain with lemon and black pepper. However, if you like a sauce with them, this is one that is not so strong as to overwhelm the delicate flavor of the oysters. Serve it cold, in a bowl, and dip the oysters into it.

- 1 teaspoon olive oil
- 1 teaspoon Tabasco sauce
- ½ teaspoon Worcestershire sauce
- 1 teaspoon finely chopped chives
- 1 shallot, finely chopped
- ½ teaspoon parsley, finely chopped
- ¼ teaspoon white wine vinegar
- fresh ground white or black pepper

Combine all the ingredients in a bowl, chill, and serve. Enough for 2 dozen oysters.

Oyster Cocktail

This is a mild cocktail sauce for oysters. It also goes well with clams. If you cannot get oysters on the half shell, but only already shelled and sold in a container, don't despair, use this compromise recipe.

- 2 dozen oysters
- juice of 1 lemon
- 3 drops Tabasco sauce
- 1 teaspoon Worcestershire sauce
- ½ teaspoon tomato puree
- freshly ground black or white pepper

Drop the oysters, with their juice, into individual serving bowls. Combine the other ingredients, season to taste, and add to the oysters and their juice. Turn them in the sauce so that they are well coated. Keep chilled until ready to serve.

Note: You can also serve a small bowl of fresh horseradish as a dip for the oysters.

Mussels

The type of mussel most commonly found has a long shell with a very slight roughness along the back. It is smaller than the oyster. In Belgium and France mussels, just like oysters, are often eaten raw, on the half shell with lemon. Unless you are very sure that the mussels you buy come from unpolluted waters (and nowadays these are rare places) it is wiser to steam them until they come open. Never eat the ones whose shells have opened unsteamed. They must be tight shut (and they are almost as hard to open as oysters). Like oysters, only eat them during the months with an "r".

Sea Urchins

Most popular in Europe these are now available in some parts of the United States. They have a very unpleasant bristly shell, covered with spines, but inside they are small, pinkish-yellow and delicate. They are slit opened, washed in salted water, and eaten raw out of the shell. They are delicious.

Smoked Salmon with Anchovy Butter

Serve this hors d'oeuvre with thin slices of toast.

Anchovy butter
4 slices thin toast
4 slices smoked salmon
4 slices lemon
parsley sprigs to garnish

Make the anchovy butter according to the directions in Salad Dressings and Sauces and spread it on the toast. Put the slices of salmon on the toast and garnish with lemon and parsley. Serves 4.

Smoked Salmon Rolls Stuffed with Cream Cheese

8 thin slices smoked salmon
1 cup cream cheese
kosher salt and freshly ground black pepper
2 tablespoons horseradish
1 tablespoon paprika
parsley to garnish

Trim the salmon into rectangles about 1½ inches by 3 inches. In a bowl combine the remaining ingredients, except parsley, and mix well. Wrap a salmon square around about 1½-2 tablespoons of the mixture and secure with a toothpick. Place the rolls on a dish and garnish with parsley. Makes about 16 rolls.

Eggs Stuffed with Shrimp

12 shrimp, extra small
lemon juice
4 hard-boiled eggs
½ cup mayonnaise
kosher salt and freshly ground black pepper
1 teaspoon chopped parsley
½ teaspoon cayenne pepper

Shell, devein, and wash the shrimp and let them marinate in the lemon juice for two to three hours. Cut the eggs in half and remove and beat the egg yolks with the mayonnaise and seasonings. Dry the shrimp and add them to the egg-mayonnaise mixture, making sure they get thoroughly coated. Place them in the indentations of the egg whites and sprinkle with parsley and cayenne pepper. Serves 4.

Shrimp with Olives and Feta Cheese

This dish is an attractive addition to a smorgasbord. Take a large plate and arrange the shrimp with the olives, cheese, hard-boiled eggs, or any other garnishes that might go with this combination (chunks of smoked ham are a good addition).

1 pound shrimp
lemon juice
1 pound Greek feta cheese
½ pound black Greek olives
4 hard-boiled eggs

Shell the shrimp, wash and marinate them in lemon juice for a couple of hours (or until they turn pink) in the refrigerator. When ready to serve place on a large dish with the olives, the cheese (cut into one inch-chunks) and the hard-boiled eggs, halved or quartered. Decorate with parsley and serve.

Note: If you cannot get feta cheese use any crumbly soft white cheese as a substitute.

Marinated Mushroom and Sardine Canapé

2 cans sardines
¼ pound mushrooms, chopped
olive oil
1 teaspoon finely chopped parsley
1 teaspoon finely chopped chives
1 teaspoon Dijon mustard
2 teaspoons capers
kosher salt and freshly ground black pepper
dark bread

Combine the oil from the sardines with the mushrooms and add extra olive oil, if needed, to be absorbed by the mushrooms. Refrigerate at least an hour. Mash the sardines and combine with the herbs and mustard, and add some of the capers, chopped. Add the mushrooms and mix together thoroughly. Spread on rounds or squares of dark bread and top with the remaining whole capers.

Curried Sardine Canapé

2 cans sardines
1 teaspoon sugar
1 teaspoon curry powder
⅓ cup cream
lemon juice to taste
2 tablespoons chopped onion
2 tablespoons chopped apple
kosher salt and freshly ground black pepper
dash nutmeg
dark bread

Mash the sardines in their oil, add the other ingredients and mash together. Season and spread on rounds or squares of dark bread. Crack a little extra black pepper over the top for decoration.

Steak Tartare Balls

Prepare Steak Tartare according to direction in the section on Meat and mix in all the ingredients, including the egg yolks, capers, parsley, and onions, but use only half the suggested amount of chopped onion. Otherwise the flavor of the walnuts may be overpowered.

Steak Tartare
white of egg
chopped parsley
chopped walnuts

Shape the Steak Tartare into balls and dip each into white of egg. Roll the balls in the parsley and walnuts and place on a serving dish. Makes about 12–15 balls.

Marinated Raw Beef with Foie Gras

French dressing
12 very thin slices raw beef, cut against the grain
1 small can pâté de foie gras
kosher salt and freshly ground black pepper
parsley to garnish

Make a French dressing (see the section on Salad Dressings and Sauces) and marinate the beef in it for about two to three hours. Pat dry, season, wrap around foie gras and secure roll with toothpicks. Garnish with freshly chopped parsley. Enough for 6.

Fish and Shellfish

To many of us the idea of eating raw fish is still a bit strange. However, raw fish has been a favorite for centuries in Scandinavia, Latin America, and Polynesia, and is especially prized among the Japanese, whose method of preparing and serving it is now becoming extremely popular among Westerners.

Unfortunately most fish served in the United States is either boiled, grilled, or fried, and this is hardly surprising as supermarket fish rarely lends itself to anything else. Most fish in mass-market outlets have been, or are, frozen, and for raw-fish recipes simply won't do. To serve good, fresh fish you must go to the fish market — or catch it yourself.

To recognize fresh fish first look at the eyes. They should be bright and protuberant rather than dull and opaque. The flesh should be stiff, not limp, and the smell fresh rather than "fishy." Shellfish should have tightly closed shells and feel heavy.

Sashimi (Japanese Raw Fish)

Sashimi as the Japanese call it, should be very fresh — never frozen — and preferably a salt-water fish. It is not marinated but it is cut in a certain way and served with cold vinegared rice (*sushi*), fresh ginger, *wasabi* (green horseradish paste), and soy sauce as a dip. It does not taste at all fishy.

Use fresh tuna, squid, porgy, sea bass, striped bass, red or blue snapper, or abalone. Fillet the fish and remove the bones.

There are several different ways of cutting the fish. (The flesh is firm and is easy to cut.) Slice a tuna against the grain, much as you would a loaf of bread. The slices can be thick, paper thin, or in cubes. Thin slices are placed over little mounds of rice and served as individual portions. Thicker slices can be placed over the rice in a large serving dish, as can cubes. White meat fish should be filleted and placed on a board. Then cut it against the grain into paper-thin slices, which you can further cut into thin strips.

Sashimi and Sushi Wrapped in Nori

Nori is a dried seaweed which you can buy in Japanese stores. It comes in sheets. To make the *nori* soften so that you can wrap it easily around the *sushi* (vinegared rice) and *sashimi*, pass it over a gas flame or candle.

This dish is a meal in itself. Serve with *wasabi*, fresh ginger, and soy dips (see index).

Sushi

- 3 cups cooked rice
- 2 tablespoons white vinegar
- 1 tablespoon sugar
- 2 tablespoons sake or 1 tablespoon dry sherry
- kosher salt to taste

Run cold water through the cooked rice. Mix together other ingredients and pour over rice. Toss and refrigerate until ready for use.

On a flat board place the strips of *nori*. Put enough rice in the strip to cover, place *sashimi* inside that. You can put a dab of *wasabi* on the *sashimi*. Then roll the *nori* over the ingredients into a flat cylinder. Cut it into sections about 1 to 1½ inches long. This method is easy but the first few times you probably won't get perfect cylinders. Place the sections base up on a serving dish.

Note: This is a good dish to serve in smorgasbord or as an hors d'oeuvre.

Serve the fish immediately (and keep it refrigerated right until you prepare it). Put the condiments into little serving bowls on the table. See index for suggested dipping sauces to go with *sashimi*.

Sashimi is filling and besides the rice needs only a light salad. These fish dishes can also be served as hors d'oeuvres.

Salmon

Salmon that is to be eaten raw should first be marinated. Cut it in half lengthwise and remove the bones. Then place fish, skin side down, in an enamel or pyrex dish and put weights over it. Refrigerate for two or three days, turning the fish from time to time.

Salmon with Dill (Gravlax)

1½ pounds fresh salmon, boned and scaled
kosher or sea salt
2 tablespoons sugar
freshly ground white pepper
1 bunch fresh dill

Prepare fish for marinating as above. Place one half of the fish, skin down, in a deep dish. Mix together salt, sugar, and pepper and spread over fish. Chop the dill coarsely and work into the fish flesh. Cover with other half of the fish, place aluminum foil on top and add weights to press it down. Refrigerate for two to three days, turning the fish every twelve hours.

Remove fish from marinade, scrape it and wipe dry with paper towels. Place it, skin side down, on a chopping board and slice thinly in slices about 1½ inches thick, removing the skin from each slice.

Arrange in serving dish with lemon slices and parsley. Serve with toast and the Mustard Sauce described in the section Sauces and Salad Dressings. Serves 4.

Hawaiian Lomi Salmon

1½ pounds fresh salmon, boned, scaled and refrigerated for two or three days
kosher salt and freshly ground white pepper
½ cup vinegar—white wine, cider or tarragon
2 medium Bermuda onions

Dry marinated salmon, remove skin and slice. In deep dish mix seasonings with vinegar. Place fish slices in vinegar, turning to make sure that they are thoroughly coated. Slice onions in strips and place in mixture. Leave at room temperature for about ½ hour.

Salmon Salad

1½ pounds fresh salmon, boned, scaled, and refrigerated as described above.
kosher salt and freshly ground white pepper
juice of half a lemon
4 hard-boiled egg yolks
4 tablespoons pitted and chopped black olives
1 tablespoon finely chopped capers
½ cup freshly made green mayonnaise

Dry marinated salmon, remove skin and slice. Place slices in dish with seasonings and lemon juice. Meanwhile prepare egg yolks, olives, capers, and mayonnaise. Place these in bowl with salmon and toss, making sure the slices are coated evenly with the mixture. Serve with toast.

Salmon with Mushrooms

The salmon must be marinated two or three days. It is then sliced and tossed in a dressing with the mushrooms. This is an excellent luncheon dish or as the main course for a summer dinner. Toast is a good accompaniment.

1½ pound fresh salmon, prepared according to Salmon with Dill
½ pound fresh mushroom caps
kosher salt and freshly ground black pepper
2 tablespoons olive oil
1 tablespoon red pepper
1 tablespoon green pepper
Fresh green mayonnaise with 1 tablespoon chopped dill added
2 drops Tabasco sauce

Arrange the skinned, sliced salmon in a dish and refrigerate. Slice the mushroom caps. Place in a bowl, season, and pour the oil over them. Toss so that they absorb the oil (they are even better left in the oil overnight). Chop the peppers finely. Prepare a green mayonnaise according to the directions in the section Salad Dressings and Sauces, adding the extra dill, and to it add the peppers and Tabasco sauce. Adjust seasoning. Toss the salmon and the mushrooms in the mixture and serve. Serves 4.

Salmon and Cucumber Salad

1½ pounds fresh salmon, marinated, boned, and scaled
1 cup sour cream
juice of half a lemon
1 tablespoon chopped chives
1 tablespoon finely chopped onion
1 tablespoon chopped fresh dill (optional)
2 cucumbers
1 small head Boston lettuce
kosher salt and freshly ground black pepper

Slice the fish in pieces about ¾ inch to 1 inch thick. In a large bowl combine the sour cream, chives, onion, and dill. Put salmon slices into the mixture and toss. Chill for an hour. Slice the cucumber and salt the slices; refrigerate until ready for use. After about one hour, dry the cucumber and add to the salmon-sour cream mixture. Season and serve over Boston lettuce leaves. Serves 4–6.

Pickled Salmon, Turkish-Style

1½ pounds fresh salmon, boned, and scaled
kosher or sea salt
2 tablespoons sugar
2 tablespoons vinegar
1 tablespoon olive oil
freshly ground white pepper
1 bay leaf
2 cloves garlic, crushed
2 tablespoons husked pistachio nuts
1 tablespoon whole black peppercorns
1 teaspoon fresh minced parsley
1 teaspoon fresh minced tarragon (or dried if fresh is not available)

Prepare fish and rub salt into the flesh. In a bowl mix the remaining ingredients and work into the fish flesh. Place one half of the fish skin side down in a deep dish. Cover with the other half, place aluminum foil over the top, and put weights on it to press it down. Refrigerate for two or three days, turning every twelve hours in its juices.

Remove the fish from the marinade, scrape and wipe dry with paper towels. Place skin down on chopping board and slice it thinly about 1½ inches thick. Remove the skin from each slice.

Arrange in a serving dish and garnish with parsley, tarragon, and lemon slices. Serves 4.

Serve with a Sauce Niçoise or Horseradish Cream sauce.

Marinated Fillet of Fish

Use any white fillet of fish for this dish (porgy, sole, snapper, flounder, striped bass, etc.) except cod or halibut.

- 1½ pounds white fillet of fish
- ½ cup lemon juice
- kosher salt and freshly ground white pepper

You can either fillet the fish yourself or buy already filleted meat. Wash and dry it and leave it in the marinade for at least a day.

When the fish has been marinated, dry it and cut it into slices 1½ inches thick. Serve with homemade mayonnaise, fennel mayonnaise, or one of the other sauces listed in the section Salad Dressings and Sauces.

Fish Marinated in Limes

- 1½ pounds raw fish (any kind except cod or halibut)
- 1 cup fresh lime juice
- 2 Bermuda onions, thinly sliced
- 6 tablespoons olive oil
- 3 tablespoons vinegar
- kosher salt, freshly ground white pepper

Bone the fish and cut it into slices about 1½ inches thick. Cover with lime juice and leave to marinate overnight in a deep enamel or pyrex dish, covered. Remove from juice. In a bowl combine onions, oil, vinegar and seasonings. Pour over fish and serve. Serves 4.

Sole with Spicy Marinade

You can use any fresh white fish except cod or halibut with this marinade. The lemon and lime juice "cooks" the fish when it is left to marinate for a few hours. Serve with baked sweet potatoes or corn.

- 4 fish fillets
- 1 cup fresh lime juice
- 1 cup fresh lemon juice
- 4 dried chilis, seeded and pulverized (use blender or pestle and mortar)
- 1 clove garlic, squeezed
- kosher salt and freshly ground black pepper
- 2 red onions
- parsley sprigs

Wash and dry fish. Mix ingredients for marinade together and pour over fish. Refrigerate, turning occasionally in the marinade, for two to three hours. When ready serve garnished with onion rings and fresh chopped parsley. Serves 4.

Fish Fillet Salad with Horseradish

- 2 pounds fish fillets (use a white fish such as sole, whitebait, etc. not cod or halibut)
- juice of 1 lemon
- 2 tablespoons olive oil
- 4 tablespoons horseradish
- 1 pint sour cream
- 1 onion, chopped
- 2 tablespoons white wine vinegar
- 2 tablespoons chopped dill
- kosher salt and freshly ground white pepper
- 1 head Boston lettuce
- 2 hard-boiled eggs
- 3 tomatoes
- chopped dill

Wash and dry the fillets, place in a deep dish, and cover with lemon juice and oil. Leave for about two hours to marinate. In a bowl combine the horseradish, cream, onion, vinegar, dill, salt, and pepper. Mix well. Remove fish from marinade and slice in strips about ½ inch thick. Mix into the cream sauce and refrigerate for another hour. When ready, serve on lettuce leaves and garnish with sliced hard-boiled egg, sliced tomato, and chopped dill. Serves 6.

Fish with Limes and Coconut Milk

- 1½ pounds raw fish (not cod or halibut)
- 1 cup fresh lime juice
- 1 coconut
- ½ clove garlic
- kosher salt and freshly ground white pepper

Clean, bone, and slice the fish into slices 1½ inches thick. Place slices in a heavy enamel or pyrex dish and marinate in lime juice overnight. Grate the coconut into its own juice, squeeze in garlic, and season. Remove fish from the marinade and dry it, then pour the coconut mixture over it. Serves 4.

Raw Fish Fillet Salad

- 2 small fish fillets (any kind except cod or halibut)
- 2 celery stalks, finely chopped
- 1 grated carrot
- 2 large grated radishes
- ½ cup sliced raw mushrooms
- 1 Romaine lettuce

Dressing

- 2 egg yolks
- 1 tablespoon dry sherry (or sake)
- 1 tablespoon vinegar
- 1 tablespoon lemon juice
- ½ teaspoon sugar
- 2 tablespoons olive oil
- 1 tablespoon fresh chopped parsley
- kosher salt and freshly ground white pepper

Wash and slice the fish fillets into thin strips. Place in salad bowl with vegetables (tear the lettuce into bite-size pieces). In another bowl mix the dressing. Taste, adjust seasonings, pour over vegetables and fish, and serve.

Marinated Red Snapper

- 1½ pounds red snapper, cleaned and filleted
- 1 cup lime or lemon juice
- kosher salt and freshly ground white pepper
- 1 Bermuda onion, chopped in thin strips
- 1 medium tomato, skinned and chopped
- 1 green pepper, chopped
- 1 cucumber, peeled and chopped
- 1 hard-boiled egg, chopped

Cut fish into slices about 1½ inches thick. Place strips in heavy enamel or pyrex dish and marinate in lime or lemon juice and seasonings for an hour and a half. When fish has marinated remove from juice. Garnish with vegetables and egg and serve with a little paprika scattered over the top for decoration.

Mackerel with Black Olives

- 2 Boston mackerel
- kosher salt
- 1 cup lemon juice
- 1 tablespoon finely chopped parsley
- ½ cup pitted and chopped black olives
- spicy soy dip

Clean, split, and bone the mackerel. Leave the skins on. Place skin down in a deep enamel or pyrex dish. Salt and pour over lemon juice. Marinate, covered, overnight. Dry and slice, with skin on, removing the thin outer film, into pieces 1½ inches thick. Place in a serving dish and garnish with parsley and olives. Mix together ingredients for spicy soy dip according to directions in Salad Dressings and Sauces and serve on the side in a dip dish.

Herring Salad

- 3 herring (you can use salt, pickled or Bismark herring, too)
- ½ cup cucumber, coarsely chopped
- 1 cup cooked kidney beans, drained and cooled
- 1 cup cooked beets, chopped
- 1 cup cooked potatoes, diced
- ½ cup black olives, pitted and chopped
- 1 lettuce, shredded
- 1 grated carrot

Dressing

- 4 tablespoons olive oil
- 1 tablespoon tarragon vinegar
- 1 teaspoon dry mustard
- kosher salt and freshly ground black pepper

Clean and bone herring and chop into chunks about 1 inch square. Put all ingredients into a salad bowl. In another bowl mix the dressing. Adjust seasoning, pour over salad, and serve.

Tunafish with Hard-Boiled Egg

- 1½ pounds tunafish
- 3 hard-boiled eggs
- ½ cup walnuts
- 1 tablespoon capers, drained and chopped
- 2 teaspoons chives
- 1 teaspoon grated fresh ginger
- 1 teaspoon dark mustard
- ½ cup sour cream

Garnish

- Green horseradish paste (*wasabi*, a powder available in Japanese and health food stores)
- soy sauce

Wash and dry the tuna and cut into slices 1½ inches thick, cutting it against the grain. Chop the eggs and walnuts and place in large bowl with capers, chives, ginger, mustard, and sour cream. Mix together and place in shallow serving dish. Arrange the fish slices over the mixture. Serve with horseradish paste and soy sauce in dip dishes.

Mackerel in Japanese-Style Vinegar Dressing

Serve this fish with Sushi (cold vinegared rice) and a salad of raw carrots.

1½ pounds mackerel
kosher salt
1 cup white vinegar (rice vinegar if available)
1 cup cold water
2 tablespoons sugar

Make sure that the mackerel is clean and that the fins, etc. have been taken off. There is a thin tough film over the skin which you should remove after the mackerel has been marinated. It pulls off easily leaving the skin intact but not so tough. Salt the fish well on both sides and place it skin down in an enamel or glass dish. Cover and refrigerate overnight. Combine the vinegar, water, and sugar in a dish and place the mackerel in the liquid. Leave covered to marinate for half an hour at room temperature. When ready to serve remove from marinade and place on a chopping board. Cut the fish in half and slice it diagonally in strips about an inch wide. Serve immediately. Serves 4.

Mackerel and Artichoke Hearts A La Grecque

1½ pounds fresh mackerel
1 jar artichoke hearts in oil or 1 can artichoke hearts and 3 tablespoons olive oil
1 tablespoon chopped capers
1 tablespoon white wine vinegar
½ clove garlic, crushed
1 teaspoon chives, chopped
1 teaspoon parsley, chopped
kosher salt and freshly ground black pepper

Marinate the mackerel in salt overnight as in the previous recipe. When ready to serve place on cutting board and slice diagonally in strips about one inch wide. In a bowl combine the oil from the artichokes (or 3 tablespoons olive oil) and mix with the vinegar. Add the chopped capers, garlic, chives, parsley and season. Place the mackerel in a dish and arrange the slices with the artichoke hearts. Pour over the sauce and garnish with parsley sprigs and whole capers. Serves 4. (This recipe can be prepared in advance and refrigerated until needed.)

Mackerel with Basil

1½ pound fresh mackerel
kosher salt
2 tablespoons fresh chopped basil leaves
juice of 2 lemons
mustard sauce (with 1 tablespoon chopped basil instead of dill)
freshly ground black pepper

Remove the tough outer film from the mackerel skin (you can do this after it has been marinated if you prefer). Salt the fish well on both sides and rub the salt into the flesh. Add the leaves and the lemon juice and make sure that the fish is covered with the liquid. Marinate overnight. Prepare a mustard sauce according to the directions in Salad Dressings and Sauces. Half an hour before serving remove the fish from the refrigerator, turn in the marinade, and leave at room temperature. When ready to serve remove from marinade and place on chopping board. Cut the fish in half and slice diagonally in strips about an inch wide. Sprinkle pepper over the slices and garnish with fresh basil. Serves 4.

Pickled Herring Scandinavian

2 cups finely chopped herring
1 cup finely chopped apple
3 cups cooked beets, chopped
½ cup finely chopped dill pickle
4 tablespoons finely chopped dill
1 tablespoon tarragon vinegar
1 Bermuda onion, chopped
parsley sprigs

Dressing

3 hard-boiled eggs
1 tablespoon Dijon mustard
½ teaspoon dry mustard
2 tablespoons white wine vinegar
¼ cup olive oil
4 tablespoons heavy cream
kosher salt, freshly ground black pepper

Dip Sauce

1 cup sour cream
2 tablespoons beet juice
2 teaspoons lemon juice
1 teaspoon chopped chives

In a large bowl combine fish, apple, beets, pickle, onion, and dill and toss in vinegar. In another bowl combine the hard-boiled egg yolks, mustard, and vinegar. Add oil, stirring fast with a fork. Add cream and continue to stir until the dressing is thick. Pour over herring mixture and place in a shallow serving dish. Scatter chopped egg whites over the top for decoration and garnish with parsley sprigs. Beat sour cream, beet juice, and lemon juice together. Season and put in small serving dish with chives scattered over the top for decoration.

Salt Herring Salad

1 salt herring (any other herring can be substituted)
1 cup freshly chopped apple
1 cup cooked chopped potatoes
1 grated carrot
1 cucumber, peeled and diced
juice of half a lemon
1 tomato, diced
2 small onions, diced
fresh basil, chopped
1 head lettuce
2 teaspoons capers, drained and chopped
kosher salt and freshly ground black pepper

Dressing

1 cup sour cream
lemon juice
¼ cup tarragon or white wine vinegar

Soak salt herring in water (change frequently to remove salt). Remove skin and bone. Cut into small pieces and place in salad bowl. Add other ingredients, season well and toss. In another bowl make dressing and pour over salad and serve.

Grapefruit and Crabmeat Salad

Raw crabmeat goes well in this salad, but to use it you must buy a live crab and kill it yourself. Otherwise use canned or cooked crabmeat. If you use raw crabmeat, run it under cold water and marinate in lemon juice for one or two hours.

1 grapefruit
2 cups Chinese cabbage, shredded (or white cabbage)
2 cups crabmeat
1 cup mayonnaise
2 tablespoons lemon juice
2 tablespoons dry white wine
kosher salt and freshly ground white pepper

Peel the grapefruit and remove the membrane from the sections. Place in bowl with shredded cabbage and crabmeat. Make a mayonnaise according to the directions in Salad Dressings and Sauces and add to it the lemon juice, wine, and seasonings to taste. Pour over the salad and serve. Serves 4–6.

Shrimp

Raw shrimp are more juicy and have more flavor if they are marinated in lemon juice for several hours. Choose tiny, fresh shrimp and wash them well in salted water. They should have no smell and should be springy when you pull their tails back. Peel them before you marinate them. During the marinating they will turn from a translucent gray color to pink, which indicates that they have been "cooked" in the process.

I am indebted to Raeford Liles for introducing me to this shrimp dish and to the Kamehachi Sushi restaurant in New York City where I first tasted raw shrimp and many other superb raw fish dishes.

Tomatoes Stuffed with Marinated Shrimp

1 pound shrimp, washed and shelled
juice of 2 lemons
4 large firm ripe tomatoes
1 cup mayonnaise
1 teaspoon cayenne pepper
1 teaspoon fresh chopped parsley
kosher salt and freshly ground black pepper
2 teaspoons fresh chopped dill (optional)

Marinate the shrimp in the lemon juice for three to four hours, so that it is pink. Hollow out a cavity in the tomatoes, reserving the tomato meat for use another time. Salt the cavity. Make a mayonnaise sauce according to the directions in Salad Dressings and Sauces. Remove the shrimp from the marinade, add seasonings to mayonnaise, chop the shrimp coarsely, and turn in the sauce. Fill the tomatoes with the mixture, sprinkle a little cayenne pepper over the top, and decorate with sprigs of parsley. Serves 4.

Shrimp Salad

Before you begin to make the salad, marinate the raw, peeled shrimp in lemon juice until they turn pink, about four hours.

3 cups marinated shrimp
1 cup fresh oysters, drained (or 1 can oysters, drained)
1 tablespoon finely chopped chives
2 tomatoes, peeled and diced
1 cucumber, peeled and diced
1 cup homemade mayonnaise or 1 cup commercial mayonnaise plus a raw egg yolk
1 teaspoon curry powder
1 tablespoon lemon juice
kosher salt and freshly ground black pepper to taste

Remove the shrimp from the marinade and toss together with the other ingredients in a large bowl. Serve on lettuce leaves and scatter finely chopped parsley over the mixture at the end for decoration. Serves 4.

Lobster

Raw lobster is delicious but the worst part of preparing it yourself is killing it. Lobsters tend to hold out as long as possible before they give in and die thereby using up all their resources and the meat becomes dry and tasteless. For this reason lobsters are kept alive in water until the last minute. When you choose a lobster make sure it is one with a good hard shell. Lobsters shed their shells to allow for growth and one with a soft shell will often have a small amount of meat.

Since we are talking here about eating lobster raw, the traditional method of plunging the lobster into hot water cannot be used. However it is worth mentioning that contrary to what many people believe it *is* cruel to put the lobster into rapidly boiling water. This has been demonstrated by tests carried out in England and America. Shellfish, when afraid or in great pain, will throw a claw, the intent being to decoy the enemy. Lobster and crab often throw a claw when they are put in boiling water, but if you put them into cold water and bring it very gradually to the boil they faint before they feel pain.

The other method of killing lobster, without cooking it, is to pierce the spinal cord. Hold a cloth over its back and tail and drive a knife through the whitish cross that is indented in the center of the main section of carapace. You will kill it instantly and painlessly. If the lobster gives a thresh of the tail while you are holding it don't let it go. If it falls on to the floor the shell could break and this would give intense pain to the animal.

After you have killed one lobster, the rest is easy. To some people the idea of eating lobster raw may seem strange, but the Japanese have been doing it for centuries. The flesh is firmer and more juicy when eaten this way and it keeps its taste which is often boiled out from it when it is cooked. Rice and Japanese-Style Raw Salad are good accompaniments.

1 live lobster, about 1½ lbs
2 teaspoons finely grated ginger
2 teaspoons fresh grated horseradish
raw seaweed as a garnish (optional)
soy sauce, served separately as a dip

Kill the lobster and remove the meat. Run it under cold water until the flesh is firm. Boil the shell until it is red and replace the flesh into it when it has cooled. Put the ginger and the horseradish into little serving dishes, garnish the lobster with the seaweed and serve at once, with soy sauce. Serves 2.

Lobster with Basil

3 lobsters
juice of 2 lemons
1 cup mayonnaise (preferably homemade)
1 tablespoon finely chopped onion
3 tablespoons finely chopped celery
3 tablespoons coarsely chopped fresh basil
1 tomato
1 teaspoon fresh chopped parsley
1 hard-boiled egg, sliced

Kill the lobster by plunging a knife into the spinal cord and run the meat under cold water until it is firm. Place it in a dish and squeeze the lemon juice over it. Leave it to marinate while you prepare the mayonnaise and seasonings. If possible leave it for a couple of hours. To the mayonnaise add the onion, celery, and basil. Mix well. Remove the lobster meat from the marinade and mix in the dressing. Garnish with slices of tomato, parsley, and sliced egg. Serves 4–6.

Meat

Raw meat should be fresh and should be eaten right away. When you buy it, avoid the supermarket and go to your local butcher. It is always better to have the butcher grind the meat in front of you and make sure that he removes as much fat as he can. Beef should be red and marbled with little veins of fat. If the meat has a damp look to it, it means it has been frozen. Lamb should have very pale pink flesh (the paler it is, the younger the lamb).

Chicken unfortunately is now produced in such a mechanical way that it is almost tasteless. The meat used in raw chicken is the breast. It can be made juicier and more tasty if it is boned and pounded with a knife before you cut it up. Never buy frozen chicken for eating raw (and remember, most supermarket chicken has been frozen at some time).

Steak Tartare

This is a great French favorite and can be made in a variety of ways. Always buy the best sirloin and have the butcher grind it in front of you.

Mix the ingredients into the steak and make a hole in the center for the raw egg yolk. Garnish with onions, capers, and parsley. Serve in individual portions.

Master Recipe

2 pounds ground sirloin
dash cumin
dash cayenne
dash curry powder
¼ teaspoon thyme
½ teaspoon powdered mustard
dash Tabasco sauce
dash Worcestershire sauce
Cognac or Port to taste
dash soy sauce
kosher salt and freshly ground black pepper

Garnish

4 egg yolks
2 tablespoons drained capers
4 teaspoons chopped parsley
2 tablespoons chopped onions

Combine all ingredients in bowl, tasting until you have reached the seasoning you like. Divide the mixture into four patties, making a hole in the middle for the egg yolk. Serve on individual plates, garnished with capers, parsley and chopped onion.

Steak Tartare with Anchovies

To the master recipe add 2 tablespoons of chopped anchovies with their oil. You can also add finely chopped green olives and pimientos.

Steak Tartare with Caviar

To the master recipe add 2 egg yolks, 1 tablespoon capers, 1 teaspoon parsley, and 1 tablespoon chopped onions. Spread over thinly buttered fresh black bread and top with a generous spoonful of fresh black caviar. Squeeze lemon over the top, garnish with parsley and serve.

Steak Tartare Rolled Over Leeks

To the master recipe add 2 egg yolks, 1 tablespoon capers, 1 teaspoon parsley and 1 tablespoon chopped onion. Meanwhile marinate four small cooked leeks in a sauce vinaigrette. Roll out the meat gently into squares about 5 x 5 inches. Place a leek in each square, season, roll the meat over and scatter parsley over the top. Serves 4. (Directions for preparing sauce vinaigrette may be found in the section Salad Dressings and Sauces.)

Chopped Steak Viennoise

The raw meat is garnished with a sour cream and chive sauce and is good served on toast.

2 pounds ground meat
1 teaspoon paprika
½ teaspoon celery seed
dash nutmeg
dash curry powder
1 tablespoon chopped onion
2 teaspoons lemon juice
1 tablespoon olive oil
kosher salt and freshly ground black pepper
¾ cup sour cream
2 tablespoons chives

In a bowl combine the meat and all the ingredients *except* the sour cream and chives. Adjust seasoning. In another bowl mix the sour cream and chives, season and serve separately with the meat. Serves 4–6.

Marinated Flank Steak

Serve this with hot potatoes and cooked vegetables, or serve it as part of a smorgasbord or salad spread, or with a cucumber and yoghurt salad.

1 pound flank steak
3 tablespoons olive oil
1 tablespoon wine vinegar
1 tablespoon soy sauce
1 tablespoon fresh ginger
1 tablespoon chopped onions
kosher salt and pepper

Slice flank steak thinly against the grain. Mix dressing in bowl and pour over flank steak. Marinate for an hour. Serve in marinade with ginger and onion as a garnish. Serves 4.

Beef Strips in Sauce Vinaigrette

The steak is marinated in garlic and oil for about an hour before being tossed in the sauce. This dish is excellent either as a main course served with hot or cold vegetables or as an hors d'oeuvre served with toast. If you serve it as an hors d'oeuvre, use half the amount.

1 pound good steak, no fat on it
1 clove garlic
3 tablespoons olive oil
kosher salt and freshly ground pepper
sauce vinaigrette

Slice the steak thinly against the grain. In a bowl, squeeze the garlic clove (or chop finely if you have no squeezer). Add the oil and seasoning, using a liberal amount of black pepper. Let it marinate for about an hour. Make a sauce vinaigrette according to the directions in the section on Salad Dressings and Sauces substituting one tablespoon Dijon mustard for the garlic called for in the recipe. When ready to serve, toss the steak in the sauce and garnish with parsley sprigs and whole capers. Serves 4.

Beef in Horseradish Cream Sauce

This dish goes very well with cooked potatoes and Apple and Beet Salad. You can also serve half the quantity as an hors d'oeuvre with black bread. Beer is a good accompaniment.

1 pound beef steak, no fat on it
3 tablespoons olive oil
1 clove garlic
1 teaspoon Dijon mustard
1 teaspoon chopped parsley
horseradish cream sauce
kosher salt and freshly ground black pepper

Slice the steak thinly against the grain. Combine the oil, garlic (squeezed or finely chopped), and mustard. Mix well, season, and toss the slices in the mixture. Leave to marinate for about an hour. Meanwhile prepare the horseradish sauce according to the directions in Salad Dressings and Sauces. Remove the beef slices from the oil, drain, and add to the horseradish sauce. Scatter parsley over the top and serve. Serves 4.

Minced Lamb

To us the idea of raw lamb may seem strange but it is certainly no more peculiar than steak tartare and in the Middle East it is eaten all the time. Of course the lamb must be fresh, non-fatty and should be ground before your eyes.

1 cup crushed wheat cereal
¾ pound lean lamb, finely ground
½ teaspoon prepared Dijon mustard
freshly ground nutmeg to taste
dash allspice
dash cayenne
1 teaspoon finely chopped fresh mint or basil
kosher salt and freshly ground black pepper
1 small onion, finely chopped
½-⅔ cup olive oil
chopped fresh parsley to garnish

Soak the wheat in cold water for about 10–15 minutes. Drain it in a colander lined with a cloth. Wrap the cloth around it and squeeze it dry. In a large bowl combine the wheat with the lamb and spices and knead until well mixed in and smooth. Adjust seasoning. To serve divide into 4 portions and make a hollow in the center of each (as you would for steak tartare). In each opening put oil and garnish with the chopped onions and parsley. Serves 4.

Breast of Chicken

This is a popular Japanese dish. It can be eaten as an hors d'oeuvre, as a light luncheon dish with rice and a salad, as part of a buffet, or as part of the main course of a meal with perhaps a small cooked dish to go with it (such as scampi, cold veal or pork, or grilled fish).

4 chicken breasts
kosher salt

Garnish

2 cucumbers
Soy sauce as a dip
Wasabi paste (green horseradish)

Wash and dry the chicken breasts. Pound them with the flat side of a heavy knife. Bring a pan of water to the boil. Turn off the heat. Cut the breasts into pieces about 1 inch square. One by one dip them quickly into the hot water so that they just whiten on the outside. Place them in a bowl and refrigerate. Peel and shred two cucumbers and put them in a bowl of ice cold water until you are ready to serve them. Place the chicken on a serving plate, garnish with cucumber. Serve the horseradish and soy sauce in separate dishes.

Vegetables

The nutritional value of raw or partially cooked vegetables is twice as great as that of cooked ones. When you buy vegetables to eat raw, look for the young, tender ones. The smaller ones have much more flavor than large, tough, overgrown vegetables. When you are buying leafy vegetables make sure they are firm and crisp.

Have a wooden chopping board and a sharp knife to cut the vegetables.

Some vegetables are better when they are "parboiled" or blanched. This means that they will absorb a dressing more easily and germs will be destroyed. You can do this in two ways: either drop the vegetables into boiling water for a few seconds (the best way to do this is to put them in a large sieve and put it in the water as you would dip French fries) or put them in a colander and pour rapidly boiling water over them. The latter method is good for less tough vegetables (such as bean sprouts).

Unless you have your own garden and can grow your vegetables organically you will have to wash them thoroughly before you eat them. Sprays have become so dangerous nowadays and are being used in such profusion that it is not safe to eat any fruit or vegetable without washing it well. Dry leafy vegetables with paper towels and let them sit in the refrigerator to get crisp before serving. A dressing will not stick to wet leaves.

Apple and Beet Salad

This is good in a cold buffet or smorgasbord.

- 1 cup cooked, or 1 small can, beets
- 2 raw, crisp apples
- squeeze of lemon
- 2 celery stalks
- 2 tablespoons finely chopped walnuts
- 4 tablespoons olive oil
- 1 tablespoon red wine vinegar
- kosher salt and freshly ground black pepper

Drain the beets (save the juice for use in soups or as a flavoring) and slice them. Peel,core and dice the apples, squeezing lemon juice over them to prevent discoloration. Dice the celery (save the leaves for soups and stocks). In a salad bowl combine the vegetables with the walnuts. In a small bowl mix the oil, vinegar, and seasonings and pour over salad. Serves 4.

Avocado and Orange Salad

- 1 cup fresh orange juice
- 1 teaspoon finely grated orange peel
- 1 dried red chili pepper, crushed
- 1 teaspoon grated fresh ginger
- 1 cup grated carrots
- 2 avocados
- 3 tablespoons lemon juice
- 3 tablespoons sesame oil (use olive if you have none)
- ½ cup raisins, soaked in equal amount warm water
- kosher salt and freshly ground black pepper

Combine the orange juice, orange peel, and dried pepper. Add the ginger, seasonings, and carrots and leave for an hour at room temperature. Meanwhile soak the raisins. When ready to serve slice the avocados and squeeze lemon juice over them to stop them from going brown. Add to the bowl with the oil. Add the raisins, mix well, correct seasoning and serve. Serves 4–6.

Bean Sprout Salad

- ½ pound bean sprouts
- boiling water
- soy sauce dressing

Pour boiling water over the bean sprouts, rinse in cold water and drain. Make a soy dressing according to the directions in Salad Dressings and Sauces and pour over the sprouts. Serves 4.

Broad Beans with Lemon Juice

This is a Mediterranean dish and can be served either as an appetizer or as a vegetable. Make sure that the beans are young and tender (all the better if you can get them fresh from your own garden).

1 pound broad beans, shelled
½ cup olive oil
juice of 1 small lemon
kosher salt and freshly ground black pepper
dash nutmeg (optional)

Place the beans in a dish. Mix the oil, lemon juice, and seasonings separately and pour over the beans. Serves 4.

Note: If you find the beans bitter, parboil before serving.

Grated Beetroot with Cardamom

2 small beets (raw or cooked)
1 teaspoon raw sugar
kosher salt
2 teaspoons cracked cardamom seeds
1 head lettuce
1 tablespoon chopped onion
French dressing

Grate the beets (or slice if cooked) and sprinkle sugar, salt, and cardamom seeds over them. Leave them for about an hour. Shred the lettuce and combine in salad bowl with onion. Pour over the dressing, toss, and serve. Serves 4.

Grated Beet Salad

2 small beets (raw or cooked)
3 stalks celery
1 carrot
6 baby tomatoes
1 head Romaine lettuce
kosher salt and freshly ground black pepper
French or cream salad dressing

Grate the beets (or slice, if cooked) finely and place in bowl. If you plan to use the cream style dressing, set aside a little of the grated beet to mix in the dressing; it will give it a pinkish tone. Add the celery, finely chopped, the carrots, grated, and the tomatoes, cut in half. Tear the lettuce into pieces and add. Make a French or cream style dressing according to the directions in the section on Salad Dressings and Sauces, toss and serve. Serves 4–6.

Bohemian Salad

1 head lettuce
2 small beets (raw or cooked)
2 egg yolks
½ onion, chopped
1 teaspoon Dijon mustard
1 tablespoon red wine vinegar
3 tablespoons olive oil
kosher salt and freshly ground black pepper

Shred the lettuce and place in salad bowl. Grate the beets finely (slice if cooked) and add to bowl. In a smaller bowl mix the egg yolks with the onion and mustard. Add the vinegar and mix. Gradually beat in the oil and pour over the vegetables. Mix well and serve. Serves 4.

Broccoli with Mayonnaise

The broccoli flowerets should be parboiled (dropped for a few seconds into boiling water so that they soften slightly without cooking).

1 bunch broccoli
1 cup homemade mayonnaise
kosher salt and freshly ground black pepper

After parboiling the flowerets dry them thoroughly. Make a mayonnaise sauce according to the directions in Salad Dressings and Sauces and turn the broccoli in the mixture. Season and refrigerate until ready to serve. Serves 4.

Broccoli with French Dressing

A sauce vinaigrette would also go well with raw broccoli; it is much stronger in flavor than a French dressing so be guided by what else you intend to serve with the vegetables.

1 bunch broccoli
French dressing
kosher salt and freshly ground black pepper
dash nutmeg

Prepare the broccoli according to preceding recipe. Make a French dressing according to the directions in Salad Dressings and Sauces and pour over the broccoli. Refrigerate until ready for use (preferably for a couple of hours). Before serving sprinkle nutmeg over the top. Serves 4.

Cabbage with Bean Sprouts

This salad goes well with fish dishes, particularly Japanese raw fish. Try it with a French dressing, to which you have added a teaspoon of soy sauce.

4 cups shredded cabbage
1 grated carrot
1 can bean sprouts, drained
4 diced radishes
1 green pepper, diced
1 teaspoon crushed dill seeds
1 tablespoon grated onion
kosher salt and freshly ground white pepper

Combine all ingredients in salad bowl. Pour over dressing, toss and serve.

Cabbage and Radish Salad

1 small white cabbage
1 cup sliced radishes
1 clove garlic
juice of 1 lemon
3 tablespoons olive oil
kosher salt and freshly ground black pepper

Shred the cabbage finely and place in a large bowl with the radishes. Squeeze the garlic and the lemon juice in a separate, smaller bowl. Gradually add the oil, beating until the mixture is opaque. Season and pour over the vegetables. Serves 6–8.

Red Cabbage Salad

1 small firm red cabbage
1 cup red wine vinegar
1 teaspoon raw sugar
1 cup green mayonnaise
½ cup heavy cream
2 tablespoons each chives and tarragon (fresh)
kosher salt and freshly ground black pepper

Core and finely shred the cabbage. Bring the vinegar to the boil, add the sugar, mix well, and pour over the cabbage. Leave to marinate for an hour. Meanwhile make a green mayonnaise according to the directions in the section on Salad Dressings and Sauces. Gradually beat in the heavy cream and the seasonings. Remove cabbage from marinade and toss well in the dressing. Serves 4–6.

Red Cabbage with Celery

1 small, firm red cabbage
5 stalks of celery
celery leaves
1 egg yolk
1 cup olive oil
⅓ cup red wine vinegar
½ teaspoon raw sugar
½ teaspoon dry mustard
kosher salt and freshly ground black pepper

Shred the cabbage and slice the celery stalks finely. Put the leaves to one side for garnishing. In another bowl mix the remaining ingredients, first whipping the yolk with a fork until it is light and fluffy adding the vinegar, dry ingredients and the oil a little at a time, beating constantly as you would a mayonnaise. Adjust seasoning and pour the mixture over the vegetables. Toss and serve. Serves 4–6.

Chinese Cabbage

1 small head Chinese cabbage (or white cabbage)
1 cup radishes
juice of 1 lemon
½-⅔ cup olive oil
1 teaspoon fresh thyme leaves, chopped
kosher salt and freshly ground black pepper

Shred the cabbage finely and place in bowl. Slice the radishes thinly and add. Mix the lemon juice, oil, thyme, and seasonings together. Pour over the cabbage and serve. Serves 4–6.

Mixed Coleslaw

1 parsnip, grated
2 carrots, shredded
1 cup grated white cabbage
1 cup radishes, thinly sliced
juice of half a lemon
2 teaspoons fresh tarragon
⅔ cup olive oil
kosher salt and freshly ground black pepper

Combine the vegetables in a salad bowl. Mix the lemon juice, tarragon, oil, and seasonings separately. Pour over the salad and refrigerate until ready to serve (or about one hour). Serves 4.

Carrots with Anise

This makes a good salad with fish and some beef dishes.

2 carrots
1 tablespoon anise seeds
juice of half a lemon
½ cup olive oil
1 tablespoon white wine vinegar
kosher salt and freshly ground black pepper

Grate the carrots finely. In a small bowl put the anise seeds, lemon juice, oil, vinegar, and seasonings. Mix well and pour over the carrots. Refrigerate for an hour and serve. Enough for 4.

Carrots with Lemon Juice

2 cups carrots, grated
2 tablespoons lemon juice
½ cup olive oil
1 teaspoon finely chopped parsley
kosher salt and freshly ground black pepper

In a bowl place the grated carrots. In another bowl mix the lemon juice with the oil, add the parsley, season, and pour over the carrots. Marinate for an hour in the refrigerator and serve. Serves 4.

Carrots in Mayonnaise

2 cups carrots, slivered with a vegetable peeler
1 cup homemade mayonnaise
1½ teaspoons Dijon mustard
2 tablespoons heavy cream
dash curry powder
kosher salt and freshly ground black pepper to taste
1 tablespoon coarsely chopped parsley

In a bowl place the finely slivered carrots. Make one cup of mayonnaise according to the directions in the Salad Dressings and Sauces section and to it add mustard, cream, and curry powder. Season and pour over the carrots, toss, scatter parsley over the mixture, and serve. Serves 4.

Note: This salad is particularly good during the summer with cold roasts.

Pickled Cucumber Salad

This is good as a garnish for smorgasbord, or as a side salad.

2 cucumbers
¾ cup white wine or tarragon vinegar
1 tablespoon raw sugar
kosher salt and freshly ground white pepper
2 tablespoons fresh dill

If there is wax on the cucumber skin, peel the cucumber; otherwise leave the skin on. Slice the cucumber as thinly as possible and sprinkle salt over the slices. Let stand about an hour so that the water comes out of them. In a small pan mix the vinegar and sugar over very low heat so that the sugar melts. Dry the cucumber and place it in a dish. Pour the mixture over, season, and chill. When ready to serve, garnish with coarsely chopped dill. Enough for 4.

Cucumbers in Turmeric

3 cucumbers
kosher salt
1 tablespoon fresh chopped ginger

2 tablespoons sesame oil (or peanut oil)
2 shallots, minced
1 clove garlic
1 teaspoon turmeric
1 tablespoon raw sugar
½ cup tarragon vinegar
¼ cup water
freshly ground black or white pepper

Peel the cucumbers, halve, and remove the seeds. Cut into pieces about an inch long and cover with salt. Let stand salted for about half an hour. Meanwhile prepare the dressing. In a skillet heat the oil and add the shallots, chopped garlic, and ginger. Fry quickly but don't brown. Add the remaining ingredients, stir in, and pour the mixture over the cucumbers, which you have dried. Enough for 4.

Stuffed Cucumbers with Cashews

2 cucumbers
1 tablespoon cashew nuts
2 teaspoons seedless raisins
2 teaspoons chives
2 tablespoons cream cheese
juice of half a lemon
sugar to taste
kosher salt and freshly ground black pepper to taste

Peel the cucumbers, cut in half lengthways, and scoop out the seeds with a teaspoon. Salt them and refrigerate for half an hour. Meanwhile finely chop chives, cashews, and raisins. Mash the cream cheese, mix in the ingredients, reserving a few chives. Add lemon, sugar, and seasonings to taste. Dry the cucumbers, fill with the mixture, and scatter chives over the top for decoration. Serves 4.

Cucumber and Tomatoes with Fresh Mint

2 cucumbers
3 tomatoes
½ cup chopped fresh mint leaves
kosher salt and freshly ground black pepper
French dressing

Peel the cucumbers, run a fork down the side to make a lacy effect, slice, and salt. Let stand in refrigerator for an hour. Slice the tomatoes and combine in a bowl with the mint. Dry the cucumber slices on paper towels and add to bowl. Season to taste and serve with a French dressing made according to the directions in the Salad Dressings and Sauces section.

Marinated Cauliflower with Fennel

In order to ensure that the cauliflower will absorb the marinade easily it should be dropped into rapidly boiling water for a few seconds so that it softens slightly without cooking.

1 head cauliflower
1 cup olive oil
juice of 2 lemons
1 clove minced garlic
1 tablespoon fresh fennel (or ½ teaspoon dried)
1 teaspoon chervil
½ teaspoon thyme
1 teaspoon freshly ground coriander seed
kosher salt and freshly ground black pepper

Break the cauliflower into flowerets, drop briefly into boiling water, remove, and dry. In a bowl combine the remaining ingredients, adjust seasoning, and pour over cauliflower. Marinate overnight or for at least two hours. Serves 4.

Dandelion Leaves in Orange and Soy Dressing

Choose small, young leaves and wash them carefully. Dry the leaves well and refrigerate until ready to serve.

1 pound dandelion leaves, washed and dried
½ cup orange juice
1 teaspoon grated orange peel
2 tablespoons soy sauce
1 teaspoon grated fresh ginger
3 tablespoons olive oil
1 garlic clove, squeezed
kosher salt and freshly ground black pepper

Combine all the ingredients except dandelion leaves in a bowl and mix well. When ready to serve, pour over the leaves, toss well, and serve at once. Baby tomatoes make a fine addition to this salad.

Eggplant with Olives and Hard-Boiled Eggs

This is excellent with lamb dishes or any stew or hearty meat dish. The eggplant is marinated and thus becomes tender. Choose small, young eggplants, not large overgrown ones. The latter tend to be woolly and should only be used in dishes that require long cooking in the oven.

1 small, tender eggplant, diced and salted
2 tablespoons cider vinegar
1 onion, finely chopped
fresh basil and parsley, chopped
1 cup black olives, pitted
2 hard-boiled eggs
kosher salt and black pepper
2 tablespoons olive oil

Marinate the eggplant in the vinegar for 2 hours. Combine in a dish with onion, herbs, and olives. Slice the hard-boiled eggs and set aside. Season the eggplant and turn in oil. Adjust seasoning, garnish with slices of egg, and serve. Serves 4.

Eggplant and Watercress Salad

1 small eggplant
kosher salt
red wine vinegar
1 bunch watercress
1 tablespoon chopped Spanish onion
1 tomato, sliced (optional)
¼ pound black olives
2 hard-boiled eggs, quartered
1 teaspoon fresh chopped basil
1 teaspoon fresh chopped parsley
sauce vinaigrette

Skin and chop the eggplant into small cubes. Salt well and leave for about an hour. Dry off the salt and marinate the eggplant in vinegar for about three hours. Dry and place in salad bowl. Add the watercress, onion, tomato (if desired), olives, eggs, and herbs. Mix well. Prepare a sauce vinaigrette according to the directions in Salad Dressings and Sauces and add. Toss and serve. Serves 4–6.

Endive with Roquefort Dressing

Never wash endive as this tends to make it bitter. Cut off the bottom part and discard brown outer leaves. Then take the leaves off separately, wiping any dirt away with a paper towel. Put the leaves in a bowl and pour the dressing over and serve immediately. Endive goes brown when it is exposed to the air.

4 medium-sized endives
Roquefort dressing

Prepare the dressing according to the directions in Salad Dressings and Sauces. Arrange the endive leaves in a dish and pour the dressing over them. Toss and serve. Serves 4.

Endive with Orange and Soy Dressing

This is a good dressing on endive served with veal, pork, or chicken.

4 medium-sized endives
Orange and soy dressing

Prepare the dressing according to the directions in Salad Dressings and Sauces, arrange the leaves in a dish, and pour it over them. Toss and serve immediately. Serves 4.

Fennel with Mint

1 head fennel
½ cup radishes
1 tablespoon chopped fresh mint
cream salad dressing or sauce fines herbes

Slice the fennel into thin strips. Slice the radishes and place in a bowl with the fennel. Scatter the mint over the top. If you make a cream salad dressing, add half a clove of garlic crushed into the mixture. Follow directions for dressings in Salad Dressings and Sauces. If you make the sauce fines herbes, add mint to the herbs you put in. Serves 4.

Japanese-Style Raw Salad

This delicate salad of finely grated raw vegetables goes well with grilled meats and fish. Use a vegetable peeler and grate the vegetables in thin strips. Keep them refrigerated until you are ready to serve.

1 tablespoon grated fresh ginger
2 grated cucumbers (grated longways)
2 grated carrots (grated longways)
1 large white radish, grated (or 2 tablespoons red radishes, grated)
1 medium-sized onion, grated

Dressing

1 tablespoon soy sauce
½ cup rice vinegar or distilled white vinegar
1 teaspoon sugar
kosher salt and freshly ground white pepper

In a bowl combine the grated vegetables. Mix the dressing in another bowl, adjust seasoning, toss over vegetables, and refrigerate until ready for use. Serves 4.

Japanese Radish (Daikon) and Carrot in Vinegar Dressing

This dish is a traditional Japanese accompaniment to raw fish and seafood dishes. If you cannot get the large Japanese radish the smaller white radishes will do. Failing that you can even use ordinary radishes but they will not have quite the same result.

1 large Japanese radish (or ½ pound small radish)
1 carrot
1 teaspoon raw sugar
¼ cup tarragon or white wine vinegar
kosher salt to taste

Shred the radish and carrot finely with a vegetable peeler or grater. Put in a bowl and cover with cold water. Refrigerate until ready for use. In a saucepan put the sugar and vinegar. Heat through so that the sugar melts. Season and cool in refrigerator. When ready drain water off vegetables and pour the dressing over. Adjust seasoning and serve.

Mushroom Salad with Cream

This salad goes with chops, chicken, or meat dishes that don't have cream with them. It is delicious as an appetizer too.

½ pound mushrooms
¼ cup heavy cream
1 tablespoon olive oil
1 tablespoon lemon juice
1 medium onion, grated
¼ teaspoon sugar
kosher salt and fresh ground white pepper

Slice the mushrooms and place in an enamel or pyrex dish. Cover with cream, lemon juice, and oil and toss. Leave for ten minutes so that the liquid is soaked in. Add onions and seasonings. Refrigerate until ready for use. Serves 4.

Note: This dish improves if left overnight in the refrigerator.

Salade Niçoise

One of the greatest French salads; a true one contains tunafish, anchovies, cold cooked string beans, olives, and tomatoes. Hard-boiled eggs, lettuce, peas (raw or cooked), pimiento and cucumber can also be included.

1 can tunafish
2 tomatoes
½ cup cooked beans or cooked potatoes
2 hard-boiled eggs
½ cup raw peas
¼ pound black olives
1 small can anchovies
sauce vinaigrette

Using a deep dish build up the ingredients in layers, using the oil from the canned fish. Strew the anchovies and olives over the top. Make a sauce vinaigrette according to the directions in Salad Dressings and Sauces and pour over. Toss and serve. Serves 4.

Onion and Tomato Salad

This is very popular in Spain. It is strong and harmonizes well with roast or grilled meats.

1 medium Spanish onion, sliced
3 large tomatoes
1 cup olive oil
2 tablespoons red wine vinegar
kosher salt and freshly ground black pepper

Slice the onion into rings. Slice the tomatoes in thick slices. Put the vegetables into a shallow dish. Mix the oil, vinegar, and seasonings and pour over the vegetables. Serves 4.

Dressed Onions

This raw onion dish goes well with curries, pork, and sausage dishes and in a buffet dinner. Because the onions are soaked before they are served, their strength is diminished so that they will not overpower the taste of the other dishes.

2 large Spanish onions
½ cup vinegar
2 tablespoons Dijon mustard
½ teaspoon chili powder
1 teaspoon sugar
kosher salt and freshly ground black pepper
parsley to garnish

Slice the onions and soak them in water for several hours to diminish their strong flavor. Dry them. In a bowl combine the other ingredients, adjust seasoning, and pour over the onions. Chill until ready to serve. Serves 6.

Paprika Salad

2 apples
1 stalk celery
1 large sweet orange
1 cup halved, shelled walnuts
lemon cream dressing
1 head Boston lettuce
kosher salt and paprika

Chop the apple, celery, and orange and combine in a bowl with the walnuts. Make lemon cream dressing according to the directions in Salad Dressings and Sauces and add 1 tablespoon paprika to it. Chill. When ready to serve, tear the lettuce into pieces and put in salad bowl. Add the other ingredients and scatter paprika over the top. Serves 4.

Parsnip with Cabbage

This vegetable dish is a good accompaniment for casserole dishes, pork, or any heavy main course. The Japanese always grate their raw vegetables. This means that the flavor is released and the vegetable absorbs dressing easily.

1 parsnip, grated
1 cup cabbage, shredded
1 carrot, grated
1 onion, grated
1 tablespoon tarragon, chopped coarsely
kosher salt and freshly ground black pepper
French dressing with 1 teaspoon soy sauce added

Combine ingredients in bowl and correct seasoning. Make the dressing according to the directions in Salad Dressings and Sauces and pour it over the ingredients just before you are about to serve. Serves 4.

Peas with Cucumber and Parsley

1 pound peas, shelled
2 cucumbers
3 tablespoons parsley
1 cup homemade mayonnaise
kosher salt and freshly ground black pepper
dash sugar

If you are using frozen peas, thaw and dry them. Peel the cucumber, run a fork down the sides for a lacy effect, slice them, and salt them. Let the slices stand for an hour so that the moisture escapes. Meanwhile prepare a mayonnaise sauce. Dry the cucumber, place in bowl with peas and add the mayonnaise and seasonings. Serves 4.

Peas with Lettuce

1 pound peas
1 head Boston lettuce
1 teaspoon fresh chopped chives (optional)
3 tablespoons olive oil
1 tablespoon tarragon vinegar
kosher salt and freshly ground black pepper
dash sugar

Shell or thaw and dry the peas. Wash and dry the lettuce and tear into small pieces. Refrigerate. Make the dressing and when ready to serve, pour over vegetables and toss. Serves 4.

Peas with Scallions

Follow the directions for Peas with Lettuce. You can either omit the lettuce and use only the scallions, or you can serve both. I find the combination better, as the scallions on their own tend to be a bit overpowering. Use the entire scallion, chopping it very fine and discarding any old or tough green parts.

Peas with Mint

An excellent vegetable dish for a hot day.

1 pound young tender peas
2 tablespoons fresh mint
1 teaspoon sugar
3 tablespoons olive oil
1 tablespoon tarragon vinegar
kosher salt and freshly ground black pepper

Shell the peas (you can use thawed frozen peas provided they are dried first. Petits pois are particularly good). Chop the mint and add to the peas. Make the dressing in a separate bowl, adjust seasoning, and pour over peas. Toss and serve. Serves 4.

Note: Fresh basil can be substituted for the mint, giving a slightly sharper but minty flavor.

Spinach with Roquefort Dressing

To make this an excellent dish you should use good Roquefort cheese. You can substitute blue cheese but it won't be nearly as good.

Serve the salad on its own, after the meat course.

1 pound tender young spinach
baby tomatoes (optional)
clove of garlic
Roquefort dressing

Wash and dry spinach. Place in bowl with tomatoes. Make a Roquefort dressing according to the directions in Salad Dressings and Sauces and add to it a clove of garlic, crushed. Serves 4.

Spinach Salad

1 pound young tender spinach leaves
1 onion, grated
about 6 baby tomatoes
dash nutmeg
1 clove garlic
juice of half a lemon
⅔–1 cup olive oil
kosher salt and freshly ground black pepper
fresh thyme leaves (optional)

Wash and dry the spinach leaves, refrigerate until ready to serve. In a bowl combine the tomatoes, sliced in half, and the onion. In a small bowl put the nutmeg, squeeze the garlic, add the lemon juice, oil, and seasonings. Put the spinach in the salad bowl with the onion and tomatoes, add the dressing, toss, and serve. Serves 4.

Spinach in Yoghurt Dressing

½ pound fresh young spinach leaves
1 cup yoghurt
1 tablespoon olive oil
1 tablespoon lemon juice or tarragon vinegar
1 tablespoon fresh chopped mint
1 teaspoon chopped onion
1 clove garlic, split
kosher salt and freshly ground black pepper

Combine the yoghurt, olive oil, lemon juice or vinegar, and onion. Add the mint, reserving some to scatter over the top when serving. Place the garlic in the bowl to allow the flavor to permeate the dressing (for a stronger garlic taste, squeeze a little into the mixture). Chop the spinach leaves finely and toss in the dressing. Refrigerate for about an hour. Enough for 4.

Yellow Pepper Salad

You can substitute or add a red pepper in this salad to vary the color.

3 yellow peppers
6 baby tomatoes sliced in half
½ cup sliced radishes
¼ cup red wine vinegar
¾ cup olive oil
kosher salt and freshly ground black pepper

Slice the peppers into quarters and cut in half. Put in bowl with the tomatoes and radishes. Mix the oil and vinegar separately and season. Pour over the peppers. Serves 4.

Stuffed Tomatoes

These can be served as a garnish with chops, escalopes, or as a side dish with a roast. They are also attractive on a buffet table.

4 large ripe tomatoes
1 can bean sprouts, drained
½ can bamboo shoots, diced
½ cup cooked kidney beans
1 tablespoon parsley
1 teaspoon grated onion
kosher salt and freshly ground black pepper
fresh chopped basil

Remove the inside meat and seeds of the tomatoes. Combine the other ingredients, and adjust seasoning. Stuff tomatoes with the mixture, garnish with fresh chopped basil, and serve.

Aspics & Mousses

A good aspic can be one of the most exquisite dishes in any meal. The ones you find here will serve as a main course of a luncheon or light dinner, as an hors d'oeuvre, or in a buffet dinner. Aspic is particularly good for the latter because it looks attractive and you can make it the day before.

A mousse performs the same functions as the aspic. It is also an excellent way of using up leftovers, particularly fish. Again, it plays an attractive part in the setting of the buffet or dinner table.

Simple Aspic Jelly

- 1 cup of tomato juice
- 3 cups chicken stock (or fish stock for fish aspic)
- 2 envelopes unflavored gelatin
- kosher salt and freshly ground black pepper (white pepper for fish)
- 1 teaspoon sugar
- 2 egg shells, crushed
- 2 egg whites, lightly beaten
- 2 tablespoons Cognac

Bring juice, stock, gelatin (soften first in water to cover), seasonings, egg shells, and egg whites to boil. Remove from heat and stir in Cognac. Place a cloth that has been run through cold water in a sieve and strain mixture through. Place in mold and refrigerate until set.

Raw Salmon in Aspic

1 pound salmon
kosher salt and freshly ground white pepper
1 bunch fresh dill
1 tablespoon sugar
Aspic prepared according to master recipe, using fish stock
3 hard-boiled eggs
1 tablespoon pitted, chopped black olives
1 tablespoon capers
1 Boston lettuce

Cut and bone salmon. Place fish in heavy enamel or pyrex dish. Cover with salt, pepper, and half the dill and work ingredients into the flesh. Cover with foil paper, place weights over the top and refrigerate overnight. Prepare aspic using master recipe. Cut salmon into thin slices, removing the skin. Cut the hard-boiled eggs in half. In mold put about 1 cup of the aspic and refrigerate until nearly set. Then place the halved eggs in a pattern on the aspic and decorate with dill and olives. Pour over more aspic, just to cover and refrigerate again until nearly set (use freezer to speed this up). Place salmon slices, with dill and capers, on the next layer, pour over rest of aspic and refrigerate until set. To serve, turn aspic out onto arranged leaves of lettuce. Serve with mayonnaise, green mayonnaise, or mustard sauce (see Salad Dressings and Sauces).

Avocado and Watercress in Aspic

Aspic prepared according to master recipe
2 avocados
juice of half a lemon
1 bunch watercress
1 small onion, grated
½ cucumber, diced
1 stick celery, diced
kosher salt and freshly ground black pepper

Refrigerate a cup of aspic in a mold until set. Peel and pit the avocados and cut them in slices. Remove aspic from refrigerator and arrange a layer of avocado over it. Squeeze some lemon on the avocado, place some watercress between the slices, add more aspic and refrigerate again. When lightly set, add more avocado slices, watercress, and the rest of the vegetables, diced. Squeeze remaining lemon juice over the vegetables, season, and add remaining aspic. Refrigerate until set. To serve, turn out into cold dish.

Cauliflower and Chicken in Aspic

- Aspic prepared according to master recipe
- ½ head cauliflower
- 2 cups cooked chicken, diced
- 2 tablespoons cheddar cheese, grated
- 1 tablespoon sour cream
- 1 teaspoon dark mustard
- dash curry powder
- 1 tomato, cut in slices
- kosher salt and freshly ground black pepper

Prepare aspic and place 1 cup in mold. Refrigerate until lightly set. Break the cauliflower into flowerets. In bowl combine chicken, cheese, sour cream, mustard, and curry powder. Mix well and season. Cut tomato into slices. Season. Place cauliflower interspersed with slices of tomato to form a pattern, over aspic. Pour in enough aspic to cover and refrigerate once more. When nearly set add chicken mixture arranged with any remaining cauliflower. Season well, pour in rest of aspic and refrigerate until completely set. Turn out into cold serving dish and serve, garnished with parsley or watercress.

Chicken in Aspic

4 chicken breasts
¾ cup chicken broth
aspic prepared according to master recipe with ¼ cup soy sauce, in place of tomato juice
1 cucumber
1 cup shelled peas
juice of half a lemon
kosher salt and freshly ground white pepper
Wasabi paste and soy sauce as dips

Wash and dry the chicken breasts. Pound them with the flat side of a heavy knife. Bring a pan of water to the boil. Meanwhile cut the chicken into pieces about 1 inch square. One by one dip them into the water so that they are lightly scalded on the outside and whiten. Put them in a dish and refrigerate. Prepare the aspic. Peel the cucumber and run a fork down the sides. Cut about ⅓ of it into thin slices. Put enough aspic in a mold to cover the surface and refrigerate until set. Add the cucumber slices, arranging them so that they will form an attractive pattern. Pour in some more aspic and refrigerate. When set add the peas, lemon juice, and seasonings to the remaining aspic, add the chicken and pour into the mold. Refrigerate until set (about three or four hours). Prepare Wasabi paste according to the directions in Salad Dressings and Sauces, and serve separately. Horseradish cream sauce and soy sauce also go well here.

Shrimp in Aspic

1 pound shrimp
Aspic prepared according to master recipe
3 hard-boiled eggs
1 tablespoon fresh chopped chives
kosher salt and freshly ground black pepper
lettuce leaves and fresh chopped parsley to garnish

Marinate the raw, washed, and shelled shrimp in lemon juice for about four hours, until they turn pink. Prepare the aspic and line the mold with about ¼ inch of it. Refrigerate until set (put it in the freezer and it will take only a few minutes). Chop up the eggs and put them in with the chives. Pour more aspic over to about 2 inches. Again, refrigerate. When firm add the shrimp and the rest of the aspic. Season and refrigerate until set. To serve, turn out the contents onto a serving dish and garnish with lettuce leaves and parsley. Serves 4.

Sole with Aspic

4 fillets of sole
1 tablespoon chopped shallot
1 cup olive oil
½ cup white wine or tarragon vinegar
1 tablespoon fresh chopped tarragon leaves
kosher salt and freshly ground white pepper
1 can anchovy fillets
1 tablespoon chopped gherkins
2 hard-boiled eggs, chopped
1 tablespoon beets, chopped
1 tablespoon tarragon, chopped
Aspic prepared according to master recipe

Place the fish fillets, cut into slices, in a deep dish and add the shallot, oil, vinegar, tarragon leaves, and seasonings. Work into the fish flesh and marinate overnight (or for at least four hours). Slice the anchovies into thin strips. Place the marinated fish on a serving dish and garnish with the anchovies, gherkins, eggs, beets, and tarragon. Add chunks of aspic to the serving dish and serve with green mayonnaise, prepared according to the directions in Salad Dressings and Sauces.

Fish Fillets with Aspic

You can either serve these in the jelly with mayonnaise as a sauce, or serve the mayonnaise over the fish and garnish with chunks of aspic. This dish is good as a main luncheon or summer dinner dish, or as an appetizer, using half the amount.

4 white fish fillets
1½ cups fresh lemon or lime juice (or both)
1 tablespoon chopped onion
1 can anchovy fillets
¼ pound green olives, pitted
1 tablespoon capers
2 hard-boiled eggs
1 head lettuce
chive mayonnaise
Aspic prepared according to master recipe
kosher salt and freshly ground white pepper

Slice the fillets and marinate for at least four hours in the lemon juice with the onion. Slice the anchovies into thin strips and chop up the olives, capers, and hard-boiled eggs, reserving a few whole capers and olives for garnishing. Prepare chive mayonnaise according to the directions in Salad Dressings and Sauces and the aspic. Either refrigerate the aspic with intention of serving it separately in chunks or put a little in the bottom of the mold, refrigerate, add some olives, capers and hard-boiled egg, chopped, refrigerate until set, and then add the fish and the rest of the ingredients. Leave until set. Shred the lettuce, pour the mayonnaise over it, and set the aspic in the center. If you are serving the jelly separately combine all the ingredients with the mayonnaise and garnish with the jelly chunks, extra capers and olives. Serves 4–6.

Tunafish Mousse

1 envelope unflavored gelatin
¼ cup cold water
½ cup boiling water
½ cup mayonnaise
1 tablespoon lemon juice
1 small grated onion
½ teaspoon Tabasco sauce
dash cayenne
kosher salt and freshly ground black pepper
2 cups canned tunafish
1 tablespoon chopped capers
½ cup heavy cream

Soften the gelatin in the cold water and add the boiling water to melt it. Cool. Place in bowl with mayonnaise, lemon juice, onion, Tabasco, and seasonings. Put in refrigerator until chilled to a slightly thick consistency. Beat in tuna and capers. Beat heavy cream until whipped and add to bowl. Turn into an oiled mold and refrigerate until set. Turn out on a cold plate to serve.

Salmon Mousse

- 1 envelope unflavored gelatin
- ½ cup boiling water
- 1 cup homemade mayonnaise
- juice of 1 lemon
- dash Tabasco sauce
- dash Worcestershire Sauce
- 1 tablespoon finely chopped onion
- kosher salt and freshly ground black pepper
- 2 large cans salmon
- 2 tablespoons chopped capers
- ½ pint heavy cream, whipped
- lemon sour cream dressing

Soften the gelatin in ½ cup boiling water. Cool and meanwhile make the mayonnaise. To the mayonnaise add all the ingredients except the salmon, capers, and cream. Add the gelatin and cool in the refrigerator until set slightly. Mash the salmon and add with the capers. Fold in the whipped cream and pour the mixture into a mold. Chill until set. Serve with lemon sour cream dressing, following the directions in Salad Dressings and Sauces, to which you have added 2 tablespoons fresh chopped dill. Serves 6.

Salad Dressings and Sauces

Apart from the vegetables for a salad, which must be fresh and crisp, the other factor that contributes to a good salad is the dressing. The oil you use for a salad must be good olive oil. Some people prefer to mix the dressing directly on the salad, coating the leaves with the oil first. Others prefer to mix the dressing separately and pour it on just before serving. Never put the dressing on leaf vegetables until just before you serve.

Fresh herbs are excellent in salad dressings and for information on them turn to the chapter on Herbs and Spices.

The sauces here correspond to recipes in the book and I have given suggestions of dishes to go with them. Most of them will keep in the refrigerator for a few days in a sealed container.

The butters that are listed are excellent as a base for sandwiches and canapés as well as accompaniments for fish and meat dishes.

French Dressing

1½ tablespoons tarragon vinegar
6 tablespoons olive oil
squeeze of lemon
garlic, crushed into the oil and removed before serving
kosher salt and freshly ground black pepper

Mix ingredients together and pour over salad when ready to serve.

Sauce Vinaigrette

This sauce is excellent for cold artichokes, avocado pears, cold fish dishes (including raw fish), and salads.

2 tablespoons tarragon or red wine vinegar
6 tablespoons olive oil
squeeze of lemon
1 garlic clove crushed into the oil
1 tablespoon capers, drained and chopped
1 tablespoon fresh parsley, chopped
1 tablespoon shallots or spring onions, chopped
kosher salt and freshly ground black pepper

Mix all ingredients together in bowl, taste, and correct seasoning. Serve either in a separate dish with serving spoon or pour over ingredients and serve.

Sauce Fines Herbes

This sauce is excellent for salads of all kinds, and is spicy.

½ teaspoon Dijon mustard
1 teaspoon paprika
fresh chopped basil, parsley, thyme, tarragon, whatever you have
1 tablespoon tarragon vinegar
6 tablespoons olive oil
1 clove garlic, crushed
kosher salt and freshly ground black pepper

Combine ingredients in bowl, adjust seasoning, and serve on tossed salad.

Anchovy Dressing

This dressing will keep in tightly sealed jar, refrigerated, for several weeks. It can be used with fish, hors d'oeuvres, and as a flavoring in salad dressings and sauces.

1 small can anchovies
juice of half a lemon
½ teaspoon dry mustard
1 teaspoon Dijon mustard
1 teaspoon paprika
dash cayenne
½ cup olive oil plus remaining oil from anchovies
2 chopped scallions
freshly ground black pepper

Chop the anchovies and either grind them in a mortar or put in blender. In a bowl squeeze the juice of half a lemon, the mustards, paprika, and cayenne. Add the oil gradually, mixing it well. Add the anchovy puree and blend in (either use the blender to mix entire sauce or do it gradually in a bowl). Add the scallions and adjust seasoning.

Cheese Salad Dressing

This dressing is particularly good over lettuce and tomato salads.

½ pound grated cheese (old cheese)
1 cup olive oil
⅓ cup red wine vinegar
1 teaspoon Dijon mustard
1 teaspoon sugar
1 teaspoon paprika
kosher salt and freshly ground black pepper
cayenne pepper

Combine all ingredients except the cheese and mix together. Add the cheese, mix well, pour over salad and serve.

Mayonnaise

Homemade mayonnaise is so infinitely much better than the commercial kind that it is well worth the effort of making it. It is not as difficult as some people have been led to believe. The trick is to get the oil absorbed enough so that the mixture becomes thick without curdling. If it curdles it means you have added too much oil or added it too quickly to be absorbed. All you need do in this case is to add another egg yolk and continue beating. The blender is a fast way of making mayonnaise without having to use a hand beater but be sure that you keep it at a fairly low speed.

2 egg yolks
1 teaspoon dry mustard
kosher salt
cayenne pepper
1½ tablespoons sharp wine vinegar
1½ tablespoons lemon juice
2 cups olive oil

Beat the yolks until they are sticky. Add the other ingredients except the oil, and beat. Then, drop by drop, add the oil, increasing the amount as you beat until the mayonnaise is thick and creamy. If using a blender, add the oil in a slow, steady stream.

Green Mayonnaise

Serve this mayonnaise with fish or as a salad dressing. It's also an excellent accompaniment for mousses and aspics.

1 cup homemade mayonnaise
1 tablespoon chopped watercress
1 tablespoon chopped spinach
1 tablespoon fresh tarragon or chervil
1 tablespoon fresh parsley
1 teaspoon lemon
kosher salt and freshly ground black pepper

Make a mayonnaise as in preceding recipe. If you have a blender or a pulverizer puree the vegetables and herbs. Otherwise chop as finely as you can. Add them with the lemon juice to the mayonnaise and mix well.

Chive Mayonnaise

This mayonnaise goes well with fish and salads. It's a little sharper than green mayonnaise.

1 cup homemade mayonnaise
2 tablespoons fresh chopped chives
1 teaspoon lemon juice
½ teaspoon Dijon type mustard

To the mayonnaise add the chives, lemon juice, and mustard. Mix well.

Fennel Mayonnaise

This is particularly good with raw fish.

1 cup homemade mayonnaise
2-3 tablespoons fresh chopped fennel
juice of ¼ lemon

To the mayonnaise add the chopped fennel and lemon juice.

Note: Chopped fresh dill can be substituted here with equally good results.

Sauce Tartare

This is a sharper form of mayonnaise and goes particularly well with either raw or cooked seafood.

2 egg yolks
1 teaspoon dry mustard
1 teaspoon dark Dijon mustard
3 tablespoons tarragon vinegar
1 teaspoon sugar
1 cup olive oil
1 tablespoon chopped capers
1 tablespoon chopped cucumber pickles
kosher salt and freshly ground black pepper

Beat the yolks until they are sticky. Add the mustard, vinegar, and sugar and beat a little more. Add the oil drop by drop until the mayonnaise is thick and creamy. Add the remaining ingredients and adjust seasoning. Refrigerate until ready for use.

Sauce Niçoise

This sauce goes well with salmon and other fish.

- 2 cups homemade mayonnaise
- 2 tablespoons tomato puree
- 1 teaspoon paprika
- dash curry powder
- 1 green pepper, diced
- 1 red pepper, diced
- 1 teaspoon fresh chopped tarragon
- 1 teaspoon fresh chopped chives
- kosher salt and freshly ground black pepper

Add the other ingredients to the mayonnaise and serve.

Roquefort Dressing

For this dressing to be as it should be you must use Roquefort cheese. If you use blue cheese it will be quite different (and not as good). One of the most common mistakes in American restaurants is to make a blue cheese dressing and call it Roquefort.

- 4 tablespoons Roquefort cheese, crumbled
- ⅓ cup heavy cream
- 2 tablespoons lemon juice
- 3 tablespoons olive oil
- kosher salt and freshly ground black pepper

Place the crumbled cheese in a mixing bowl. Whip in the cream with a fork. Add the lemon juice, mix, and gradually beat in the oil. Season.

Cream Salad Dressing

This is an old recipe that comes from my great-grandmother from Ballycastle, Northern Ireland. It is a delicious dressing on green salad and also goes well with raw cauliflower and raw tomatoes.

- 3 hard-boiled eggs
- 1 teaspoon sugar
- ½ teapoon dry mustard
- 1 tablespoon tarragon or white wine vinegar
- 2-3 tablespoons cream
- kosher salt and freshly ground black pepper

Remove the yolks from the eggs, chop the whites, and reserve to decorate salad. Rub the yolks smooth with a wooden spoon and blend in the sugar and mustard. Add slowly the vinegar and cream blending the ingredients to a smooth creamy consistency. Season and pour over salad just before serving. Garnish with egg white.

Yoghurt Dressing

This dressing is particularly good with aspics. It also goes well with hot or curried dishes.

- 1 cup yoghurt
- 1 tablespoon olive oil
- 1 tablespoon lemon juice or tarragon vinegar
- 1 tablespoon Dijon mustard
- 2 tablespoons chopped chives
- 1 clove garlic, split
- kosher salt and freshly ground black pepper

In a bowl combine yoghurt, olive oil, lemon juice or vinegar, and mustard. Add chives, reserving some to scatter over the top when ready to serve. Put the garlic in the bowl so that the flavor permeates (you can squeeze just a little into the mixture if you want a strong garlic taste). Just before serving, remove garlic, season, scatter chives over the top, and serve. Enough for four servings.

Note: Try using lime juice instead of lemon juice.

Lemon Cream Dressing

This dressing is very good on mixed vegetable salads.

- juice of half a lemon
- ¼ teaspoon grated lemon peel
- ½ teaspoon dry mustard
- 1 tablespoon raw sugar
- kosher salt and freshly ground white pepper
- 1 cup heavy cream

Combine all the ingredients and beat the cream in until thick. Chill until ready to serve.

Lemon Sour Cream Dressing

This dressing goes well with vegetable and fish salads and as a dressing for fish or poultry.

2 egg yolks
juice of half a lemon
1 cup sour cream
kosher salt and freshly ground white pepper

Whip the egg yolks with a fork until they are thick and sticky. This will make it easier for them to absorb the rest of the dressing. Add the lemon gradually and the sour cream. Season and refrigerate until ready for use.

Sour Cream Dressing

Try this dressing on cucumber salad or raw vegetables such as cauliflower, tomato, or carrots. It is also excellent with fish dishes and as a dip.

1 cup sour cream
2 tablespoons vinegar
½ teaspoon paprika
1 teaspoon chopped chives
kosher salt and freshly ground black pepper

Mix all ingredients together in a bowl, adjust seasoning and scatter a few extra chives and a dash of paprika over the top for decoration. Enough for 4.

Sour Cream and Cucumber Sauce

This sauce goes especially well with raw salmon, raw shrimp and any cooked fish.

1 cup sour cream
1 large cucumber
2 tablespoons fresh chopped dill
1 tablespoon chopped onion
kosher salt and freshly ground white pepper

Put the sour cream in a large mixing bowl. Peel, seed, and finely chop the cucumber. Add to the bowl with the chopped dill and chopped onion. Season and refrigerate until ready to use.

Soy Sauce Dressing

This dressing accompanies Chinese or Japanese vegetables. It is light and slightly salty. Use sesame oil if you can. It is more expensive than other oils and harder to find but worth the extra effort and the price. Don't oversalt the dressing; soy sauce itself is very salty. Sesame salt may also be hard to find (except in health food stores) but it gives a delicious nutty flavor to the dressing.

1 tablespoon soy sauce
2 teaspoons white wine vinegar
½ cup sesame or peanut oil
½ teaspoon raw sugar
sesame salt (if available) and freshly ground black pepper

Mix all ingredients together in a bowl. Pour over salad and serve.

Spicy Soy Dip

Serve this with marinated mackerel or sashimi.

½ cup soy sauce
¼ cup grated icicle or Japanese white radish
2 scallions, finely chopped including green part
1 grated carrot
1 tablespoon dry sherry or sake

Mix all ingredients and chill until ready to serve.

Orange and Soy Dressing

This dressing is strong and goes well with green vegetables such as Romaine lettuce, dandelion leaves, and spinach.

½ cup orange juice
1 teaspoon grated orange peel
2 tablespoons soy sauce
1 teaspoon grated fresh ginger
3 tablespoons olive oil
1 garlic clove, squeezed
kosher salt and freshly ground black pepper

Combine all the ingredients in a bowl and mix well. When ready to serve, pour over the vegetables and serve at once.

Avocado Sauce

This sauce is made on the same lines as Guacamole, but is thinner. It is good for fried foods, salads, and Mexican dishes.

- 2 avocados
- 1 small onion, finely chopped
- 1 green chili, chopped
- 1 medium-sized tomato
- 1 tablespoon chopped parsley
- juice of half a lemon
- kosher salt and freshly ground black pepper
- dash cayenne pepper

Peel and pit the avocados. If you have a blender, place in with onion and chili. If not place in bowl. Drop the tomato for a few seconds in boiling water so that you can peel the skin off. Take out the seeds, chop it up, and add with the parsley, lemon, and seasonings to the ingredients in the blender or bowl. Either blend or mash the sauce until smooth. Adjust the seasoning, place in a dish and squeeze lemon over the top to prevent discoloration. Scatter a little cayenne over for decoration.

Spicy Avocado Sauce

Serve this hot sauce with grilled meats, as a dip for meat hors d'oeuvres, and with chicken dishes.

- 1 large avocado
- 1 hard-boiled egg
- 1 tomato
- 1 fresh (or dried) finely chopped, seeded chili pepper
- 1 green pepper, chopped
- ½ cup olive oil
- 2 tablespoons red wine vinegar
- 1 teaspoon parsley
- ½ teaspoon coriander seed, pulverized
- 1 teaspoon chopped parsley
- kosher salt and freshly ground black pepper
- lemon juice
- cayenne pepper

Peel and pit the avocado and place in blender (if none, then mash in bowl). Coarsely chop the egg and add. Drop the tomato into boiling water, peel and pit, chop, and add. Add all the rest of the ingredients except the lemon juice and cayenne pepper. Blend at high speed (if you are mixing by hand chop *all* ingredients very finely). Place in bowl, squeeze lemon juice over the top to prevent discoloration, sprinkle cayenne over for decoration, and serve.

Brazilian Pepper and Lemon Sauce

Use this sauce for cooked meats or raw fish.

- 4 Tabasco peppers, drained and chopped
- 1 chopped onion
- 1 clove garlic, squeezed
- ½ cup lemon juice
- kosher salt and freshly ground black pepper

Combine all ingredients. Adjust seasoning, cover, and refrigerate until ready for use. Enough for 4 servings.

Cheese and Chili Sauce

This sauce is excellent on potatoes or rice or served with cooked meats. It also goes well with cooked vegetables such as broccoli or cauliflower.

- 1 cup grated soft white cheese
- ⅔ cup heavy cream
- 1 chili pepper, chopped and seeded
- 1 onion, chopped
- 1 teaspoon dried chili pepper
- juice of half a lemon
- 1 teaspoon turmeric
- ½ teaspoon cumin
- 2 tablespoons olive oil
- kosher salt and freshly ground black pepper
- cayenne pepper

In the blender combine all the ingredients except the cayenne pepper (or chop everything very fine and mix in bowl). Blend at high speed and adjust seasoning. When serving, scatter a little cayenne over the sauce for decoration.

Horseradish Cream Sauce

This is good with herring, raw fish, and raw beef. Serve in a separate dish.

- 3 tablespoons grated horseradish
- ¾ cup heavy cream
- 3 tablespoons white wine vinegar
- 2 scallions, chopped
- kosher salt and freshly ground white pepper

Combine ingredients and mix until smooth. Adjust seasoning and serve.

Wasabi (Green Horseradish)

This is excellent with any raw fish. It tastes much like very hot Chinese mustard. You can buy the powder in any Japanese store.

1 teaspoon *wasabi*
Cold water to make thick paste

Mix the wasabi with water until it is thick (just as you would make powdered mustard). Let is stand for 15 minutes before using.

Salsa Cruda (Hot Tomato Sauce)

This sauce is hot! It is a spicy sauce from Latin America and is good with cooked meat, raw and cooked fish, poultry, and Mexican dishes.

4 large ripe tomatoes
1 green *chili serrano*
1 onion, chopped
1 tablespoon coarsely chopped parsley
½ teaspoon sugar
kosher salt and freshly ground black pepper

Drop the tomatoes into boiling water for a few seconds and peel. Take out the seeds, chop finely and place in bowl. Add the other ingredients and adjust seasoning. Chill until ready to serve.

Salsa Verde (Hot Green Tomato Sauce)

This sauce is made the same way as *salsa cruda* except that green tomatoes are used instead of ripe red ones. The green sauce goes particularly well with fish.

Mustard Sauce

This sauce goes particularly well with raw salmon and raw mackerel.

3 tablespoons Dijon mustard
1 teaspoon powdered mustard
1 tablespoon finely chopped dill
2 tablespoons cider or white wine vinegar
¼ cup peanut or olive oil
kosher salt and freshly ground black pepper

Make the sauce slowly, as you would a mayonnaise, adding the oil to the other ingredients, beating as you pour.

Raw Applesauce

Use good juicy apples. Dry spongy ones may turn out all right when they are cooked, but for this uncooked sauce you need the real thing.

4 apples, medium sized
apple cider
juice of half a lemon
dash nutmeg
dash powdered cinnamon
kosher salt to taste

Peel and core the apples, slice coarsely, and put in the blender. Add a little cider and blend. Add the lemon juice and seasonings and blend, adding cider until you have reached a consistency that seems right to you.

Garlic Butter

This goes especially well with roast lamb.

1 stick unsalted butter
1 clove garlic
1 teaspoon freshly chopped parsley (optional)
kosher salt and freshly ground black pepper

Whip the butter in a bowl, squeezing the garlic into it. Add the parsley and season to taste. Refrigerate until ready for use.

Horseradish Butter

This goes especially well with roast beef and as a spread for raw fish and raw meat canapés.

1 stick unsalted butter
2 tablespoons fresh grated horseradish
kosher salt and freshly ground black pepper

Whip the butter in a bowl with the horseradish. Add seasonings to taste and refrigerate until ready for use.

Butter Maître d'Hôtel

Use this butter on fish, or as a spread on raw meat, fish, and vegetable canapés.

1 stick unsalted butter
2 tablespoons chopped parsley
1 tablespoon lemon juice
kosher salt and freshly ground black pepper

Whip the butter in a bowl, add the parsley and the lemon juice and beat until the lemon juice is completely absorbed into the butter. Season and refrigerate until ready for use.

Ravigote Butter

This is a mixed herb butter.

1 stick unsalted butter
1 teaspoon parsley
1 teaspoon tarragon
1 teaspoon chives
1 small shallot
½ teaspoon anchovy essence
kosher salt and freshly ground black pepper

Whip the butter in a bowl. Chop the herbs and shallot finely, mix in bowl with butter. Add the anchovy essence, season to taste, and refrigerate until ready for use.

Tarragon Butter

Excellent with cold chicken and bread and with raw meat on bread.

1 stick unsalted butter
1 tablespoon fresh tarragon leaves
1 tablespoon lemon juice
kosher salt and freshly ground black pepper

Whip the butter in a bowl. Chop the tarragon and add with the remaining ingredients to bowl, seasoning to taste. Refrigerate until ready for use.

Anchovy Butter

Use either as a sauce or on bread as a sandwich or canapé.

2 cans flat anchovy fillets
1 stick unsalted butter
1 teaspoon finely chopped parsley
½ teaspoon cayenne
dash nutmeg
freshly ground black pepper

Either put the anchovies, with their oil, into the blender, add the butter, blend, and add the rest of the ingredients, or beat the anchovies to a paste, and add the butter and proceed as above. Put the mixture through a sieve and refrigerate until ready for use.

Sardine Butter

Use either with raw fish as a garnish or on toast or bread as a canapé or appetizer.

1 can sardines
1 stick unsalted butter
1 teaspoon chopped fresh parsley
1 tablespoon lemon juice
dash nutmeg
dash cayenne
kosher salt and freshly ground black pepper

Remove the sardines from their oil and pound them to a paste. Whip the butter and add the sardine paste and the other ingredients. Adjust seasoning. Put the mixture through a sieve and refrigerate until ready for use.

Tomato Butter

This goes well with fish and on toast or bread, garnished with fresh basil.

1 stick unsalted butter
2 tablespoons tomato puree
kosher salt and freshly ground black pepper

Leave the butter out to soften. Mash in a bowl with the tomato puree and season. Mold into a shape and chill until ready for use.

Peanut Butter

The worst thing about this peanut butter is that it is almost impossible to stop eating it once you've started. It keeps indefinitely in a tightly sealed jar in the refrigerator. Apart from being excellent on black bread or in sandwiches it is also good as a base for sauces (particulary good with tongue).

- 1 pound raw unshelled peanuts
- about ½-¾ cup peanut oil
- kosher salt and freshly ground black pepper

Shell the peanuts (a long and arduous process) and put them in the blender. Add a little oil and continue blending and adding oil until you have a smooth paste of the right consistency. Season and refrigerate.

Mint Chutney

Use this chutney with curries and lamb dishes. It will keep in a tightly sealed jar in the refrigerator for several weeks.

- 2 tablespoons chopped fresh mint
- 1 medium-sized onion, chopped
- 1 apple, chopped
- kosher salt and freshly ground black pepper
- dash cayenne pepper
- 2 tablespoons raw sugar
- ¼-½ cup red wine vinegar

Put the onion, apple, mint, and seasonings in a bowl. Heat the vinegar, add the sugar to melt it, stir well and pour over the ingredients. Pound together (it's better to do this by hand since the blender would make the mixture too liquid) and put into a jar.

Yoghurt

This is not a raw dish, but so many raw dishes require yoghurt that it seemed a pity not to include it. Anyone who has tasted the homemade variety will never buy it ready-made again. It is quite different and a hundred times better. You can add any type of flavoring you want to it once it's made and it keeps for at least six months, using a little each week as a starter for the next batch.

You don't even need a machine, although yoghurt makers can be obtained for about $10. Yoghurt cultures are available at most health food stores. There are directions on the packet.

1 package yoghurt culture
1 package dried milk
1 pint milk

Follow the directions on the package. You heat up the milk to near boiling point and let it cool to lukewarm. Add the milk powder (this will make it thicker) and stir in the culture. Put the mixture into clean pre-warmed jars, seal, and incubate overnight in warm water. If you have a yoghurt maker simply let the mixture stand in the jars overnight, with the maker plugged in. Refrigerate and your yoghurt is done.

Juices and Beverages

This chapter contains a selection of drinks and juices chosen for the simple reason that I like them. The juices are for the main part a blend of raw fruits or vegetables, many of them easy to prepare by the use of the blender. A juicer is also a good piece of equipment for someone interested in raw juices. Apart from their delicious taste, these juices contain all their natural vitamins and are extremely healthful.

I happen to dislike the practice of using a lot of sugar in punches so if you like sweet drinks you must add more yourself. When you flavor wines with lemon, woodruff, and spices, keep tasting so that you are sure the flavor does not get too strong and overpower the wine.

Where I suggest a bottle of champagne I do not mean a vintage French Champagne. Use New York or California champagne, or an inexpensive sparkling French wine.

Tomato Juice with Lemons

tomato juice
lemons
Worcestershire sauce
kosher salt and freshly ground black pepper

For one glass of tomato juice allow the juice of one lemon. Squeeze it into the juice, add dash of Worcestershire sauce and season to taste. This drink can also be improved by a touch of fresh basil, chopped into the top of the drink. Ground mace is also good in tomato juice.

Tomato Juice with Raw Liver

Use fresh raw liver (you only need about 3 tablespoons so save the rest to cook later). This is a nourishing drink, particularly for those who have chosen the unhealthy pursuit of drinking too much the night before — it's a sure cure for a hangover.

1 pint tomato juice
3 tablespoons raw diced liver
2 teaspoons lemon juice
dash Worcestershire sauce
dash Tabasco sauce
2 tablespoons powdered yeast
dash ground mace
kosher salt and freshly ground black pepper

Put all ingredients in blender (add the liver first) and blend at high speed, until smooth. Adjust seasoning and serve. Serves 2–4.

Tomato-Clam Juice with Oregano

For really top-rate results, make this with fresh clam juice and fresh oregano.

1 glass tomato juice, chilled
1 glass clam juice, chilled
juice of 1 lemon
dash Worcestershire sauce
¼-½ teaspoon freshly ground black pepper and kosher salt to taste
3 teaspoons oregano leaves

Mix the juices, add the lemon juice and season. Mix well and garnish with oregano leaves.

Mixed Vegetable Juice

3 cups tomato juice
juice of 1 lemon (with grated rind)
2 stalks celery, with leaves
1 teaspoon chopped parsley
2 teaspoons chopped tarragon (optional)
1 tablespoon coarsely chopped onion
2 tablespoons coarsely chopped green pepper (optional)
¼ teaspoon celery seed
kosher salt and freshly ground black pepper

Put about 1 cup of the juice in the blender and add the rest of the ingredients. Blend at high speed until smooth and then add the remaining juice, continuing to blend until it is well mixed in. Chill. Serves 2–4.

Apricot Juice

2 cups unsweetened apricot nectar
¼ teaspoon ground mace
dash nutmeg
1 tablespoon fresh chopped mint
raw sugar or honey

Mix all the ingredients except the sugar together (in blender if you wish) and then add sugar to taste. Chill. Serves 2.

Apricot Milk Shake

1 pound dried, pitted apricots
water to cover (about 2 cups)
2 cups milk

Soak the apricots, covered, in the water overnight. Put them in the blender with the soaking water and the milk. Blend at high speed until smooth. Chill. Serves 4.

Borani

This refreshing Pakistani drink is excellent during the summer.

2 cups yoghurt (preferably homemade)
1 quart water
peel one lemon
dash chili powder
freshly chopped mint or basil
kosher salt and freshly ground black pepper

Put the yoghurt and the water into the blender. Chop the lemon peel coarsely and add with the chili powder, mint or basil, and season. Blend at high speed and garnish each serving with a sprig of mint or basil. Enough for 6.

Cranberry-Pineapple Juice

½-¾ cup raw cranberries
1 orange
2 cups unsweetened pineapple juice
1 tablespoon fresh mint
¼ teaspoon ground cloves
¼ teaspoon freshly ground nutmeg

Put the cranberries in the blender. Squeeze the orange and add the juice. Add the pineapple juice, mint, and seasonings. Blend at high speed. Serve cold. Makes about 4 cups.

Orange-Pineapple Punch

Use fresh orange juice for this — it will give it a quite different and much better flavor than the canned.

2 cups pineapple juice
2 cups freshly squeezed orange juice
juice of 1 lemon
½ pint lemon sherbert
1 tablespoon chopped mint

In a blender put all the ingredients. Blend well and serve ice cold. Serves 4.

German May Punch

½ cup dried woodruff
2 bottles dry white wine
½ cup Cognac
1 bottle champagne
strawberries (optional)

Put the woodruff into a large bowl with the wine and let it sit for about three or four hours, or until the wine has absorbed some of its flavor, but not so long that the woodruff overpowers the taste of the wine. Add the Cognac, the champagne, and the strawberries cut in slices, and serve very cold. Enough for six (half a bottle each).

Rum Punch

This is ideal for a large party. It is not too sweet, but it is quite strong.

4 tablespoons sugar
(preferably raw sugar)
6 oranges
4 lemons
1 pint rum
1 teaspoon bitters

In a large bowl place the sugar. Slice the oranges and add. Squeeze lemons and add juice together with rum and bitters. Taste and adjust sugar, bitters, etc. Chill and serve.

Planter's Punch

jigger (or two) of rum
1 lime
dash bitters
dash nutmeg
soda

Put some crushed ice into a glass, add the rum and the juice of one lime. Add the bitters and nutmeg and fill up with soda. Some people prefer this with a little sugar or sugar syrup.

Peach Cup

6 peaches
2 tablespoons raw sugar
2 bottles chilled Moselle wine
1 bottle chilled champagne

Cut the peaches in half, throwing away the stones. Slice them and cover the slices with sugar. Let them stand about three hours. Add one bottle of Moselle and refrigerate for another hour. When ready to serve, add the other bottle of Moselle and the champagne and serve very cold in a large punch bowl. Enough for six (half a bottle each).

Cucumber Cup

1 cucumber
1 bottle chilled light red wine
1 bottle chilled champagne (or French sparkling wine)

Slice the cucumber very thin leaving the skin on. Put in a bowl with the red wine and refrigerate for an hour. When ready to serve, add the champagne. Enough for 4 (half a bottle each).

Sangría

This is a great drink for summer. You should remove the ice when you serve it so that the drink does not get diluted, but if it's very hot I don't think that it matters.

1 bottle Rioja, cold
1 liqueur glass brandy
1 orange
1 lemon
cold soda (about 2 small bottles)

Put ice in a large jug. Peel the orange and lemon and drape the peel over the sides of the jug. Slice the peeled fruits and add to the jug. Pour in the wine and brandy. Fill up with soda. Remove the ice (if desired) and serve. Enough for 2 (half a bottle each).

Bloody Mary

1 glass tomato juice, chilled
1 jigger vodka
juice of half a lemon
dash Worcestershire sauce
dash Tabasco sauce
kosher salt and freshly ground black pepper

Mix all ingredients over ice in a glass and serve cold. Not too much salt or you'll have to have several drinks before your thirst is quenched.

Note: A squeeze of garlic or ½ glass clam juice can do wonders for this drink.

Vermouth Cassis

This is a particularly fine drink during the summer, especially at lunchtime as it is light — and cold.

vermouth	soda
crème de cassis liqueur	lemon peel

You'll have to experiment a little with this to get it to your taste. Start by taking a tall glass with ice cubes and pouring in enough vermouth to fill the glass from ⅓ to ½. Then add a little crème de cassis (I don't like to add much because it becomes too sweet for my taste), fill up with soda, and add lemon peel.

Desserts

There is no better way to finish off a heavy meal than with a light dessert of raw fruit. Few people can manage heavy pastries after a large dinner and fruits are an ideal solution. You can prepare them beforehand and you don't need to worry about them during the meal.

Included here are also some raw cakes and cookies. These are made chiefly from dried fruits and nuts, blended together with honey and wheat germ. Apart from being delicious they are extremely nutricious.

When you need a liqueur for a dessert there is no need to buy a whole bottle. Most liquor stores carry miniature bottles of liqueurs for under a dollar. If you are using a very fiery liqueur, it is sometimes a good idea to set fire to it before you pour it over the dessert so that the spirit is absorbed but the taste remains.

When you are beating egg whites rub a lemon lightly round the bowl. Any grease that might have been on it will be cut and won't affect the egg whites. Beat liqueurs into eggs and cream when they start to froth.

Apple Snow

You can make this with either raw or cooked apples, and raw egg whites. Add a liqueur to it for extra flavor (use a fruit liqueur).

2 cups apple
4 egg whites
½ cup sugar
pinch salt
2 tablespoons lemon juice
sprinkle of cinnamon

If you are using raw apples, churn them to a pulp in a blender. Beat the egg whites, add the sugar, salt, lemon juice, and apples and mix together lightly. Sprinkle cinnamon over the top, chill, and serve. Serves 4.

Lemon Snow

6 lemons
½ pound sugar
1-ounce package gelatin
4 egg whites

Grate about half a cup of peel from the lemons and set aside. Combine the juice from the lemons in a saucepan with the sugar and heat gently, then cool. Dissolve the gelatin in about 1 tablespoon warm water and add with the lemon peel to the lemon-sugar mixture. Beat the egg whites until they stand up stiffly and carefully whisk into the lemon mixture. Chill for about an hour, or until ready to serve. Serves 4.

Orange Snow

4 oranges
1 lemon
¾ cup confectioners' sugar
1-ounce package gelatin
1 pint boiling water
4 egg whites

Grate the rind of one orange and one lemon and set aside. Dissolve the gelatin in about 1 tablespoon warm water. In a bowl combine the juice of the oranges and lemon, the sugar, the gelatin, and the grated peel. Mix well and let stand at room temperature for about an hour. Add the boiling water and stir until clear, strain the mixture through a fine sieve. Beat the egg whites until they are stiff and when the liquid is cool carefully whisk them into the mixture. Wet the inside of a mold with cold water, pour in the mixture, and chill overnight. Serves 4–6.

Sweet Avocado and Lime Dessert

2 avocados
3 medium-sized limes
¾ cup confectioners' sugar

Peel and pit the avocados and mash through a sieve. Squeeze the limes into a bowl with the avocado and sugar. Taste and add extra sugar if needed. Chill until ready to serve. Decorate with lime wedges and serve in individual bowls. Serves 4.

Jamaican Sweet Avocado

2 avocados
3 tablespoons raw sugar
1 glass sherry
freshly grated nutmeg
dash lime or lemon juice

Halve and pit the avocados (you can save the stone to grow a plant) and scoop the flesh out with a spoon. Mash it in a bowl with the sugar and the sherry. Put the mixture back into the skins, squeeze lemon over top to stop discoloration, scatter a little nutmeg over, and serve. Serves 4.

Bananas with Sour Cream and Brown Sugar

Excellent as a light dessert after a heavy dinner or for a luncheon dessert.

4 bananas
2 tablespoons sour cream
1 tablespoon brown sugar
squeeze of lemon

Slice the bananas and cover with cream and sugar immediately. Squeeze a little lemon over, toss. Serve at once. Serves 4.

Bananas Pureed with Rum

3 bananas
1 teaspoon sugar
lemon juice
1 cup heavy cream
¼ ounce (1 package) gelatin
1 tablespoon warm water
1 tablespoon rum
2 egg whites

Mash the bananas in a bowl, reserving about eight slices for decoration. Squeeze lemon juice over the slices to prevent discoloration. Whip the rest of the bananas with the sugar until they are liquid. In another bowl whip the cream. Fold it into the banana mixture. Soften the gelatin in the water and add. In another bowl whip the egg whites until stiff. Add the rum to the banana mixture and mix well, then add the egg whites, folding them in carefully so that they do not drop. Place the mixture in a dish, decorate with banana slices, squeezing a little more lemon on them. Refrigerate for about six hours. Serves 4.

Bananas with Wheat Germ

A really healthy dessert and to get the best you should use homemade yoghurt.

4 bananas
juice of half a lemon
3 tablespoons honey
1½-2 cups yoghurt
3 tablespoons wheat germ

Slice the bananas and squeeze lemon juice over them. Combine the honey and the yoghurt and pour over. Scatter the wheat germ over the top (you can mix it in if you'd rather) and serve. Serves 4.

Blueberries with Blackberry Liqueur

1 pint blueberries
juice of half a lemon
blackberry liqueur

Blackberry liqueur is available in most liquor stores and it only costs a few dollars a bottle. It is excellent on fruit desserts and has a particular affinity for blueberries.

Wash and drain the blueberries. Put them in a dish and squeeze the lemon juice over them. Pour over the liqueur so that it reaches all the berries. Chill for a couple of hours before serving. Serves 4.

Figs with Honey

If you can get the figs fresh and they're not too expensive, you'll find this a superb dessert and very easy to prepare. Figs are cheap occasionally, usually when they are a little overripe. In this case it does not matter and the dessert will be just as good. Underripe figs will not do.

16 ripe green figs
¾ cup honey (clear)
½ cup boiling water
¼ pint heavy cream

Cut the figs into quarters. Put the honey in a large bowl and pour the boiling water over it. Stir well so that it thins out and add the figs, turning them in the mixture. Refrigerate overnight or at least for a few hours and serve with heavy cream. Serves 4.

Figs with Kirsch

Use very ripe figs for this dish (you can use canned figs but they won't taste nearly as good).

about 12 ripe figs
kirsch (or brandy)

Prick holes all over the figs and cover them with kirsch. Just before serving, set the liqueur on fire so that it loses its harsh edge and impregnates the figs. Serves 4.

Fruit Salad

Apples, pears, and bananas are a good basis for a fruit salad. Too much orange or pineapple drowns the other fruit. Use fresh, not preserved cherries. When you cut up the fruit do it over the bowl so that the juice won't be lost. Avoid fruits such as plums and currants in a fruit salad. Lemon juice should always be sprinkled over such fruits as apple and banana to stop them from going brown. Remove cores, skins, pips and stones from the fruit before you put it in the salad. Once you have prepared the fruits put them in a large bowl and sprinkle raw sugar over them. Add a little liqueur (kirsch, curaçao, etc.) and let stand for an hour or so in the refrigerator.

Poppy seed or caraway seed sometimes makes an interesting variation in fruit salad.

Fruit Bowl

This recipe is suitable for a dinner party or occasion. Serve it with small fancy biscuits. It is especially good for entertaining because it can be prepared in advance and it is an exotic dish without being *too* extravagant. It is also a summer dish since most of the fruits are in season at that time.

- 6 peaches
- 6 apricots
- ½ pineapple
- ½ pound cherries, pitted
- 1 pint raspberries or strawberries
- ¼ cup syrup
- 2 glasses claret
- 1 glass white wine or champagne (you can use domestic champagne bought in very small bottles)
- 1 large orange

Skin the peaches and apricots (if you drop them for a few seconds in boiling water their skins will come off easily). Pit and slice. Peel and slice the pineapple and place with the peaches, apricots, and cherries in a large serving bowl. Puree the raspberries or strawberries in the blender or through a sieve. Set aside. Combine the syrup with the claret (if the syrup is too thick, warm it slightly and it will thin out) and pour over the fruit bowl. Refrigerate for about one hour. To the puree add the wine or champagne and the strained juice of the orange. Refrigerate. Just before you are ready to serve pour the mixture over the fruit bowl, toss well, and serve. Serves 6–8.

Fruit Salad with Cardamom Honey Dressing

This dressing is good over melon, strawberries, and all manner of raw fruits. If you are using fruits that are liable to discolor (such as apples or bananas), squeeze a little lemon juice over them before serving.

- 3 large apples
- 1 pear
- 1 pint strawberries
- 1 cup cubed melon
- 2 large bananas

Dressing

- ½ pint clear honey
- 2 tablespoons lemon juice
- 1 teaspoon cracked cardamom seed

Chop the fruits, place in a bowl, and chill. Beat the honey with an electric mixer until it is pale and creamy. Gradually beat in the lemon juice and the cardamom seed. Turn the fruits in the dressing until they are all coated. Serve chilled, with heavy cream to go with it. Serves 4.

Oranges Marinated in Grand Marnier

This is quite an extravagant dish, good for a smart dinner party. It is also simple to prepare. You could serve plain chocolate biscuits on the side.

4 oranges
8 tablespoons Grand Marnier
sugar to taste

Peel the oranges, using a knife so that the skin is cut away from the orange meat. Pour Grand Marnier over the orange, sprinkle a little sugar over it, and marinate at least 24 hours, turning from time to time. Serves 4.

Mixed Fruits with Rum or Brandy Sauce

The sauce is rich and should be served separately, like a custard. In Scandinavia it is often eaten on its own but I find it a bit rich for my taste.

2 bananas, sliced
lemon juice
1 cup seedless grapes, halved
½ cup chopped walnuts
1 orange, peeled and chopped
2 apples, peeled and chopped

Sauce

5 egg yolks
2 egg whites
5 tablespoons raw sugar
1½ tablespoons brandy or rum

Put the banana slices in a bowl and squeeze lemon juice over them. Add the rest of the fruit, squeezing lemon juice over the apples, and chill. In an electric mixer (or a hand mixer) blend the egg yolks, whites, and sugar to a custard. Add the brandy or rum. Serves 4–6.

Dried Fruit Compote

This is particularly good to serve in a buffet dinner, either on its own or with an accompanying dish such as a sponge dessert or light custard.

1 cup dried apricots
1 cup dried apples
1 cup dried prunes
2 tablespoons seedless raisins
1 cup dried figs
2 tablespoons lemon juice
1 tablespoon lemon rind
1 cup sweet cider

Place all ingredients in large enamel or pyrex dish. Make sure that all the fruit is covered by the cider. Refrigerate for 24 hours and serve. Serves 4–6.

Cherries in Brandy

1 pound cherries
1 pint strawberries or raspberries
confectioners' sugar
¼ cup brandy

Pit the cherries, wash them, and place them in a large serving bowl with the strawberries. Scatter confectioners' sugar over them. Add the brandy, toss the fruits in the liquid, and refrigerate at least an hour. Serves 4.

Quick Chocolate Mousse

1 6-ounce package chocolate bits
2 eggs
2–3 tablespoons strong hot coffee
3 tablespoons rum or orange liqueur
¾ cup boiling milk

Put everything in the blender and blend for a couple of minutes at high speed. Place in individual dishes and chill for about 8 hours (preferably overnight). Serves 4.

Candied Ginger with Cream Cheese

2 packages cream cheese
1 small container candied ginger, chilled

Whip the cream cheese with a fork so that it is thick and creamy. Serve a couple of ginger slices and a good portion of cream cheese per person. Enough for 4.

Grapefruit with Raspberry Sauce

This is a good, simple dessert to serve during the summer.

3 medium-sized grapefruits, halved
1 box frozen raspberries
raw sugar to taste

Chill the grapefruit halves. Put the raspberries into the blender and make a puree, adding sugar to taste. Pour over the grapefruit halves and serve. Serves 6.

Guava Shells with Cream Cheese

This is an incredibly simple Latin American dessert. It is often served with salted crackers but I prefer it without. The guava shells are very sweet and contrast well with the cream cheese.

1 can guava shells
1 package cream cheese

For each person allow about two-three guava shells and serve them on a plate with a good hunk of cream cheese.

Melon with Port

To test whether a melon is ripe smell it (it should have a strong "melony" smell) and press it at one end. It should give slightly.

Melon does not refrigerate well — the other things in the refrigerator tend to take on its flavor. It should, however, be served cold. The best thing to do is to wrap it very well and refrigerate just long enough to get cold and then serve.

If you are using a small melon, cut it in half and serve one melon for two people. If you are serving a large one, give each person a slice.

2 small melons or one large
Port

Cut the melon and remove the seeds from the cavity. Fill the cavity with port and serve. Serves 4.

Melon with Lemon or Lime

Follow preceding recipe and serve with lemon or lime slices.

Melon with Fraises des Bois

Fill the cavities with wild strawberries, a little sugar, and port or white wine. Serve cold.

Peaches with Kirsch

To skin the peaches dip them into rapidly boiling water for a few seconds and run under the cold tap. This way the skin will come off easily without the peach cooking.

- 6 ripe peaches
- 1 teaspoon confectioners' sugar
- 1 pint raspberries (strawberries or wild strawberries can also be used)
- 3 tablespoons kirsch

Core the ends of the peeled peaches and push out the stone. In a bowl combine sugar, raspberries, and kirsch. Let stand, refrigerated, for an hour or so. Place the peaches in a bowl and fill cavities with the fruit mixture. Scatter a little sugar over the top and serve with whipped cream. Serves 4.

Pineapple with Cheese

This makes an attractive dish for a dinner party since the pineapple chunks and cheese are served in the pineapple shell. You can prepare it in advance.

- 2 large ripe pineapples
- 1 cup sugar
- 1 cup sherry or kirsch
- ½ pound mild cheddar cheese
- 1 tablespoon caraway seed (optional)

Cut the pineapple in half lengthwise through the shell. Scoop out the flesh, discarding the core, chop it into cubes and place in bowl. Add sugar and sherry and marinate overnight or for a few hours. Cut the cheese into cubes the same size as the pineapple and shortly before serving, combine with pineapple cubes. Sprinkle the caraway seeds over the mixture, place in the pineapple shells and serve. Serves 4.

Pineapple with Grapes

1 pineapple
raw sugar
1 pound green seedless grapes
kirsch

Peel the pineapple and cut it into small chunks the same size as the grapes. Sprinkle the chunks liberally with sugar and let stand about one hour. Meanwhile peel the grapes. (That should take you about an hour!) Put the fruit in a bowl and pour kirsch over before serving, using your own judgement as to how much you need. Serves 4.

Note: If peeling the grapes seems too much bother for you, don't do it. The dish will not be as good but it will still be delicious.

Pineapple with Pistachio Nuts

1 pineapple
raw sugar
kirsch
2 ounces peeled plain pistachio nuts
grated peel of an orange

Peel and dice the pineapple. Sprinkle liberally with sugar and let stand for an hour. Pour kirsch over and add the nuts and orange peel. Chill until ready to serve. Serves 4.

Raspberry Cream

2 packages frozen raspberries
¼ pint cream
sugar
¼ cup Marsala

Puree the raspberries (without thawing them) in a blender with 1 cup cream and sugar to taste. Freeze until ready to serve. Whip the rest of the cream with the Marsala. When ready to serve put the whipped cream on top and decorate with spare raspberries (save a few before you blend the rest). Serves 4.

Note: If fresh raspberries are available use the recipe for Strawberry Cream.

Raspberries with Cream Cheese

This goes well with any meal. You can serve it in one large dish or individual serving dishes, but be sure to put a few raspberries on top for decoration.

2 packages frozen raspberries
1 package cream cheese
2 tablespoons sour cream

Thaw the raspberries and set a few aside for decoration. Place the rest in blender and gradually add cream cheese and sour cream. Blend until smooth and chill until ready to serve. Serves 4.

Creole Strawberries

1 pineapple
1 pound strawberries
confectioners' sugar
kirsch

Peel the pineapple and cut it into cubes the same size as the strawberries. You can cut several slices, according to how many you need, to serve the mixture on before you cube the pineapple. In a large bowl mix the pineapple cubes with the strawberries. Scatter sugar over the top, add the kirsch according to taste, and marinate in the refrigerator for about two hours. Serves 4–6.

Strawberries Cardinal

2 pints strawberries
confectioners' sugar
½ glass champagne or white wine
1 pint raspberries
1 teaspoon sugar
½ cup almonds, blanched and split

Put the strawberries in a deep dish, cover with confectioners' sugar, add the champagne, and marinate for about an hour. Put the raspberries through a sieve and add the sugar. When ready, pour the raspberry puree over the strawberries, scatter the almonds over the top, and serve. Serves 4.

Strawberries Romanoff

2 pints strawberries
juice of 2 or 3 oranges
1 tablespoon curaçao
1 pint heavy cream
1 teaspoon sugar
curaçao to taste

Put the strawberries in a deep dish and add the orange juice and curaçao. Refrigerate for about two hours. Whip the cream with the sugar and additional curaçao and pour over the strawberries. Serves 4.

Note: This dish can also be served using kirsch instead of curaçao, in which case add a little vanilla flavoring to the cream.

Strawberry Cream

2 pints fresh strawberries
confectioners' sugar
½ pint cream
3 egg whites
4 ounces sugar
¼ cup Marsala

Wash and dry the strawberries, puree in a blender or put through a sieve. Place in a dish and scatter confectioners' sugar over them. Refrigerate. Meanwhile whip the cream with the sugar and Marsala and in another bowl whip the egg whites. In a large bowl combine all the ingredients, carefully whisking in the egg whites. Refrigerate for at least three hours before serving. Serves 6.

Note: If fresh strawberries are unavailable try the Raspberry Cream recipe and use frozen strawberries.

Coeur A La Crème

½ pound cream cheese
½ pound cottage cheese
2 cups heavy cream
1 pint strawberries
pinch salt

Combine the cheese and salt in a bowl and add the heavy cream gradually, beating constantly, until the mixture is thick and smooth. Turn into a mold and refrigerate for four hours (at least). Crush the strawberries and when ready to serve, turn the mixture out on to a plate, cover with crushed strawberries, and serve. Serves 4.

Spiced Oranges

6 oranges
¾ cup red wine
4 tablespoons raw sugar
dash ground cinnamon
dash ground cloves
1 teaspoon crushed cardamom seeds

Peel the oranges, remove the pulp, and slice. Place in a shallow wide dish. In a small saucepan combine the sugar, wine, and spices and heat through to dissolve the sugar. Pour over the orange slices and chill. Serves 4–6.

Orange Jelly

This jelly is a delicious and light dessert. You can serve it plain with whipped cream (the way I like it best) or with raw fruit. You can even add pieces of orange to the jelly.

4 oranges
peel of 1 orange
¼ cup sherry
½ ounce gelatin
½ pound sugar
½ cup boiling water
1 lemon
¼ pint heavy cream

Peel one of the oranges and marinate the peel in the sherry. Dissolve the gelatin in a little cold water, put in a bowl with the sugar, and pour boiling water over to melt the sugar. When melted add the juice of the oranges and lemon, strained, Strain in the sherry. Put in a mold. When set, whip the cream with the orange peel and a little sherry to taste and serve separately. Serves 4.

Tangerines with Kirsch

Save the tangerine peel for flavoring cooked dishes (a slightly different taste from orange peel).

4 tangerines
½ cup kirsch
confectioners' sugar

Peel the tangerines and arrange the segments in a dish. Pour over the kirsch, making sure that it gets to each segment, sprinkle confectioners' sugar over, and let stand in refrigerator for at least two hours before serving. Serves 4.

Uncooked Fruit Cake

1 cup mixed, pitted, dried fruits (apricots, figs, apples, prunes, etc.)
1 cup sweet cider
2 cups whole grain bread crumbs
1 cup pitted dates
1 cup wheat germ
1 cup seedless raisins
1 cup mixed nuts (almonds, walnuts, hazelnuts, pecans)
¼ cup honey
¼ cup brandy

Soak the fruit in the cider overnight. Put it, with the cider, into the blender. Add the bread crumbs. Add the dates, wheat germ, raisins, and nuts, reserving some walnuts for decoration on the top of the cake. Add the honey and brandy. Blend everything well and turn into a deep dish. Refrigerate for about three days.

Note: You won't be able to get all the ingredients into the blender at the same time so do it in two shifts and do the final mixing in a large bowl.

Uncooked Wholewheat Wafers

This is one of the most popular of health foods and is *very* good for you. Since the wafers are dried outside, it is preferable to make them in the least polluted atmosphere possible.

1 pound wholewheat berries
water to cover
1 cup peanut oil
2 tablespoons honey
sesame seeds

Soak the berries overnight. Drain. Grind in the blender. Add the oil, mix thoroughly, and add enough cold water to make a thin dough. Roll out on a floured pastry board as thin as possible and scatter sesame seeds over. Cut into wafers and dry in the sun. Makes about 24 wafers.

Sandwiches

Sandwiches as we know them have stayed well within the Bacon-Lettuce-and-Tomato-on-Rye-with-Mayo variety and unfortunately have become as undistinguished a food as imaginable. The only people who seem to have kept the sandwich where it should be are the Danes and in most of the sandwiches here I am trying to follow their example.

These sandwiches can be used in buffets, as hors d'oeuvres, or as smorgasbord. With the addition of a slice of bread on the other side they also become portable.

In the section on Salad Dressings and Sauces there are a variety of simple butters listed that work well as a base for these sandwiches. Always butter the bread to prevent moisture from the contents soaking through and making it soggy. If you crack lettuce leaves along the stalk, they will lie flat on the bread.

Anchovy Tartines

2 small cans flat anchovies
4 hard-boiled eggs
½ cup chopped gherkins
parsley to garnish
unsalted butter
French bread
cheese

Remove the anchovies from their oil. Slice the hard-boiled eggs. Spread the butter on slices of fresh French bread and put a slice of hard-boiled egg in the middle. Arrange the anchovy slices like trellis work, fill in with chopped gherkin and parsley. Serve with cheese, either dipping the bread into the cheese if it is soft or placing a piece of hard cheese over the top. Enough for about 8 sandwiches.

Anchovies with Dill on Toast

2 cans anchovies
juice of 1 lemon
1 garlic clove, squeezed
1 tablespoon finely chopped onion
2 tablespoons finely chopped dill
1 tablespoon fresh chopped parsley
freshly ground black pepper
1 cup pimientos
toast or black bread

Put the anchovies in a bowl and add the lemon juice, beating it in gradually. Squeeze in the garlic and add onion, herbs, and pepper. Cut the pimientos into strips. Spread the mixture on the toast or bread, arrange the pimiento strips over, and serve. Enough for 4–6.

Cheese Spread

½ cup cottage cheese
½ cup cream cheese
1 stick softened unsalted butter
2 tablespoons capers
1 tablespoon Dijon mustard
1 tablespoon anchovy paste
1 tablespoon finely chopped onion
freshly ground black pepper
fresh parsley sprigs and additional capers to garnish
black bread

Put all the ingredients except the garnishes and the bread into the blender and mix well. Adjust seasoning and spread on the bread, garnishing with the parsley and capers.

Blue Cheese Sandwich

4 thick slices blue cheese, at room temperature
unsalted butter
black bread
4 onion rings
4 raw egg yolks
2 tablespoons chives

Butter the bread and place the cheese on top. Place an onion ring on each slice and put the egg yolk in the center. Scatter chives over the top and serve. Serves 4.

Caviar with Mustard and Cress Salad

The only way to get mustard and cress salad in the United States (as far as I know) is to grow it yourself. It is easy to grow and sprouts on anything from Kleenex to blotting paper. As long as you keep it moist it will grow within a week.

I do not suggest that you substitute commercially grown watercress for mustard and cress. It is not the same at all and would spoil the taste of the caviar. Forget about the salad and serve the caviar with the hard-boiled eggs and some chopped onion instead.

Real caviar is so expensive that unless you can afford to use it this way I suggest you buy lumpfish caviar which is very inexpensive.

1 medium-sized jar caviar
2 hard-boiled eggs
about half a cup mustard and cress
unsalted butter
black bread
1 tablespoon fresh chopped onion (if no mustard and cress)

Chop the hard-boiled eggs. Spread the butter on the bread and spread the caviar. Garnish with eggs and mustard and cress. Enough for about 4–6 sandwiches.

Cucumber Sandwiches with Dill

2 cucumbers
kosher salt
unsalted butter
thin slices of homemade white bread
lemon juice
2 tablespoons fresh chopped dill
freshly ground black pepper

Peel the cucumbers, run a fork down the sides to make a lacy effect when they're sliced. Slice as thinly as possible, sprinkle salt over the slices and refrigerate for an hour. Dry and sprinkle with lemon juice. Butter the bread (it must be very thinly sliced!) and add the cucumber slices. Scatter the dill over the top and sprinkle pepper over. Butter bread for the other side and make closed sandwiches. Enough for 4–6.

Herring with Raw Apple Sandwich

Use raw or pickled herring, mix all the ingredients together and spread on dark or rye bread. Make the mayonnaise before you chop the apple so that it can be coated immediately before it goes brown.

2-3 herrings, according to size
2 apples
½ cucumber
2 gherkins
3 pickled beets
1 teaspoon capers
1 teaspoon chopped chives
1 teaspoon Dijon mustard
1 cup homemade mayonnaise
olive oil
kosher salt and freshly ground black pepper
unsalted butter
dark or rye bread
anchovy fillets to garnish (optional)
parsley to garnish

Chop the herring, apple, cucumber, gherkins, and beets. Put in a bowl and add the remaining ingredients, thinning out the mayonnaise as needed with extra olive oil. Season. Spread unsalted butter on the bread and spread the mixture over. Garnish with anchovies and parsley. Enough for about 8–10 sandwiches.

Smoked Herring with Radishes and Raw Egg Yolk

about 1–2 cups smoked herring meat
butter maître d'hôtel or tarragon butter
rye or black bread
about 6–8 radishes, sliced
4 small onion rings
1 tablespoon chopped chives
about 4 raw egg yolks
kosher salt and freshly ground black pepper

Pick over the herring meat. Make the butter according to the directions in Salad Dressings and Sauces and spread on the bread. Spread the herring over and add the radishes on top. Put the onion ring in the middle, inside it place the egg yolk, sprinkle chives over the top, season, and serve. Enough for 4 good-sized sandwiches.

Smoked Salmon with Anchovy Butter

anchovy butter
about 8 slices smoked salmon
dark bread
parsley
lemon slices
freshly ground black pepper

Prepare the anchovy butter according to the directions in Salad Dressings and Sauces. Spread on dark bread and lay the salmon slices over. Garnish with parsley and lemon slices. Just before serving grind black pepper over the salmon. Enough for about 8 sandwiches.

Open-Faced Sardine Sandwich

2 cans sardines
½ stick butter
3 egg yolks
1 teaspoon chopped parsley
1 teaspoon chopped chives
1 teaspoon chopped tarragon
1 teaspoon prepared Dijon mustard
1 tablespoon tarragon vinegar
kosher salt and freshly ground pepper to taste
dark bread
lemon slices
pickled gherkins
raw or cooked shrimp (optional)

Put all the ingredients except the bread, lemon, gherkins, and shrimp in the blender or pound in a mortar. Adjust seasoning and spread on dark bread. Serve garnished with lemon slices, gherkins, and shrimp. Enough for about 8 sandwiches.

Shrimp with Lettuce and Lemon

about 10–12 small shrimp
tarragon butter
juice of 1 lemon
1 head Boston lettuce
rye or black bread
kosher salt and freshly ground black pepper
paprika

Marinate the shrimp in the lemon juice until they turn pink. Meanwhile make the tarragon butter according to the directions in Salad Dressings and Sauces. Wash and dry the lettuce leaves and crack the leaves horizontally once along their stalk so that they will lie flat. Butter the bread and put the lettuce over it. Add the shrimp, season, and sprinkle paprika to decorate. Garnish with fresh parsley and lemon wedges. Enough for 4.

Mediterranean Sandwich Loaf

This is ideal to take on a picnic. You scrape out the inside of a large French loaf and put the ingredients inside. It can then be sliced and served. You could also serve it in individual rolls.

4 tomatoes
1 medium-sized onion
3 green peppers
¼ pound black olives, pitted
2 tablespoons capers
unsalted butter
French bread

Chop up all ingredients (except bread and butter, naturally) and mix together in a bowl. Spread the butter on the bread (after removing the doughy part from inside) and fill with the mixture. To serve cut in thick slices. Enough for 4–6.

Mediterranean Tunafish Spread

1 can tunafish
1 small can flat anchovy fillets
2 tablespoons capers
¼ pound Greek olives, pitted
juice of 1 lemon
¼ cup olive oil (as needed)
freshly ground black pepper
1 tablespoon Cognac
1 green pepper
1 loaf French bread

Put tunafish, anchovies, capers, olives, and lemon juice in the blender. Blend at high speed for a couple of seconds. Gradually add the oil, blending at low speed so that the mixture thickens like a mayonnaise. Add the Cognac and black pepper. Slice the green pepper into strips. Halve the loaf of bread longways and spread the mixture generously on each side. Lay the pepper strips over the top, close the loaf, and slice. Enough for 4–6 people.

Note: This spread can also be used as a dip.

Sesame Bi Tahina

1 cup tahina paste (available at Arab or Greek stores)
2 cloves garlic, squeezed
¾-1 cup cold water
juice of 1 lemon
kosher salt and freshly ground black pepper

In a large bowl or blender combine the ingredients and mix well. Adjust seasoning and serve with Arab or black bread.

Marinated Mushrooms with Liver Paste and Bacon

½ pound fresh white mushrooms
2 tablespoons olive oil
juice of half a lemon
½ clove garlic, squeezed or garlic butter instead of plain butter
unsalted butter (if not using garlic butter)
rye or black bread
1 head Boston lettuce
about ¾ cup liver paste
4 slices bacon

Slice the mushroom caps and marinate them in the oil, lemon, and garlic for a couple of hours (overnight if possible). Spread butter on the bread (plain or garlic according to whether you used garlic to marinate the mushrooms), put lettuce leaves over, and spread with liver paste. Add the mushrooms and the bacon, the latter cut in half. Enough for 4.

Radishes with Sour Cream on Black Bread

About 20 radishes, sliced
2 tablespoons finely chopped Spanish onion
1 tablespoon vinegar
1 teaspoon raw sugar
kosher salt and freshly ground black pepper
1 cup sour cream
unsalted butter
black bread

Put the radishes and onion in a large bowl. In a smaller one put the vinegar, sugar, and seasonings. Mix together and gradually add the sour cream. Add this mixture to the vegetables and mix well. Chill for an hour. Butter the bread and spread the mixture on. Garnish with parsley sprigs. Enough for 4–6.

Watercress Spread

This spread can be used as a dip for raw vegetables or on open-faced sandwiches.

1 bunch watercress
½ cup coarsely sliced radishes
1 cucumber, peeled and sliced coarsely
juice of 1 lemon
¼ cup sour cream
kosher salt and freshly ground black pepper
½ cup cream cheese

Remove the tougher stalks from the watercress. Put it, with all the other ingredients in the blender. Blend until smooth. Refrigerate until ready for use. Garnish with watercress leaves. Enough for about 24 small open-faced sandwiches.

Herbs and Spices

Many of the dishes in this book require the use of fresh herbs. They are not always easy to find, although vegetable markets in large cities often carry them in season. But it is easy and inexpensive to grow your own. If you live in an apartment you'll find growing herbs no more trouble than growing a small houseplant. All you need is a medium-size pot with some good earth and you're in business.

I list here a directory of herbs, some of which can be grown at home easily and others which are rarely used fresh. All salads benefit from the use of fresh herbs, as do most raw fish dishes.

Some spices, including nutmeg, peppercorns, and cardamom, are much better ground just before you use them. This is particularly important for pepper. Like coffee, it loses more than half its flavor if ground in advance.

Kosher and sea salt have more flavor and texture than plain salt and with the exception of seasoning desserts, I suggest you always use one of them.

If it is absolutely impossible for you to grow your own herbs, buy fresh ones and keep them in water.

To chop herbs, put them in a cup and use scissors.

A mortar and pestle is invaluable for herbs and spices. You can get a good wooden one for about a dollar and it is great for grinding dried spices or pulverising fresh herbs.

Herbs That Can Be Grown At Home

Basil Easy to grow, it has medium-sized, wide green leaves. Water daily and occasionally remove the top leaves as well as any flowers. This herb is delicious in all salads especially cucumber and tomato, and goes well with all seafood.

Chervil A member of the carrot family, this plant has delicate flat leaves. Water daily. Use for garnishing and in salads.

Chives It is almost impossible to fail with chives. They grow long skinny stalks and are good in mayonnaise, salads, and with fish.

Dill Very easy to grow, it produces fernlike leaves. It's good in mayonnaise, with sour cream, cucumber, eggs, and salmon. You can also use it as a garnish for open-faced sandwiches.

Marjoram Belongs to the mint family and has small leaves. It is excellent in salads and meat dishes.

Mint Water every other day. Use in yoghurt, lamb dishes, salads. The leaves are like basil leaves only smaller and rougher textured.

Oregano Very easy to grow. Use in tomato, salad, and Mediterranean dishes. The leaves are small and oval shaped.

Parsley Grows very easily, like mint. There are two kinds available, curly and flat leaf. Raw parsley is said to sweeten the breath and is good for eating after garlic. Use parsley in almost anything — no kitchen is complete without it.

Rosemary Grows very easily. Use with oranges, chicken, lamb, or pork. It has thin leaves.

Thyme Very small leaves. Water regularly and use with salads, meat, and fish dishes.

Tarragon One of the most exquisite herbs. It has long thin leaves and grows easily. Use with salads, chicken, eggs, and fish dishes.

Sage Easy to grow, it has thinnish flat leaves. Use with chicken, veal, pork, and cheese.

Savory Easy to grow. Use in salads, juices, and bean dishes.

Scallions You need a large box for these. They are the seedlings of the onion. Eat them raw with salt, in salads, and in sauces.

Other Herbs and Spices

Capers These unopened flower buds are found around the Mediterranean. They are used in sauces and with raw fish and raw meat. Dry salted capers should be soaked and rinsed before they are used. They also come packed in vinegar and need no rinsing in this case.

Caraway Seeds Use these with cheese, salads, cabbage, and beets.

Cardamom The dried seeds of the cardamom plant; they are used in desserts and curries.

Cayenne A very hot red pepper ground from spices found in the Cayenne district of Africa.

Celery Seed A dish that seems to be lacking something can always be improved with celery seed. It is good in juices, salads, sauces, and with cheese.

Chili Made from ground dried Mexican peppers with other spices added.

Cinnamon The ground bark of the cinnamon tree. This spice is used in desserts (particularly apple desserts) and hot drinks.

Cloves The unopened flower buds of the clove tree, they are used to flavor desserts and drinks.

Cumin Seeds are ground and used widely in Indian and Mexican cooking. The powder is a dark mustard color.

Curry Powder This can be bought but the recipes below show you how to make your own, in either a powder or a paste. Homemade curry powder is so vastly superior to anything you can buy that it is well worth making your own. Keep it in a tightly sealed jar. You can vary the ingredients according to taste.

Curry Powder

- 2 teaspoons turmeric
- 1 teaspoon cumin
- ½ teaspoon poppy seed
- ½ teaspoon mustard seed
- 1 teaspoon fenugreek (optional if not available)
- ½ teaspoon ground ginger
- ½ teaspoon ground chili pepper
- ½ teaspoon black pepper

Grind the spices if they are whole and mix thoroughly (a blender does this very well). Put into an airtight jar. Enough for about 2 or 3 curries, depending upon how strong you like them.

Curry Paste Curry paste does not keep indefinitely. If you seal it tightly you can keep a jar in the refrigerator for a few weeks only.

- 2 cloves garlic
- 1 tablespoon fresh ginger
- ½ teaspoon ground cloves
- ½ teaspoon ground mace
- ½ teaspoon ground cinnamon
- 1 teaspoon cardamom seeds
- 2 teaspoons fresh coriander (if available)
- 1 teaspoon turmeric

Put all the ingredients in a blender or pound to a smooth paste. Put in tightly sealed jar and refrigerate until ready for use. Enough for about 2 curries.

Fennel This is a versatile plant which can be used in a variety of different ways. The bulb can be eaten raw like celery and has a minty taste. The leaves are good for flavoring fish and salads. The seeds are good in soups, and with sausage and smoked meats.

Ginger Fresh ginger is a most delicious root and can be used, thinly sliced, with raw fish, in salads, and in meat dishes. Powdered ginger is quite different and can be used with curries and desserts.

Mace This is the outer coating of the nutmeg seed and is ground and used much like nutmeg.

Nutmeg A strong seed which should be grated fresh each time you use it. Buy a miniature grater and keep it only for nutmeg.

Paprika A bright red powder that, unless it's genuine Hungarian paprika, has almost no taste and is widely used for sprinkling over dishes as decoration.

Pepper Black pepper is not as strong as white. White is used when black might spoil the appearance of a sauce, and sometimes with fish. Both should *always* be freshly ground.

Sesame Seeds These are delicious on salads and in salad dressings. There is also a good sesame salt on the market and sesame oil is excellent in salads.

Turmeric A bright yellow powder, the dried root of an orange tropical plant. It's used in curries and pickles and to give good color to sauces or mayonnaise.

Watercress Nothing beats wild watercress but unfortunately this is hard to find and the stuff on the market is nothing in comparison.

Woodruff A very sweet strong herb. It is mainly used for flavoring punches and you should be careful not to keep it in too long or you will overwhelm the taste of the wine.

Index